Stepwise Python Guide to AI and Machine Learning Beginners

Simple Explanations Projects and Workflows for Future Intelligent Software

Noah Whitman

Table of Contents

INTRODUCTION

The goal of Stepwise Python Guide to AI and Machine Learning Beginners: Simple Explanations Projects and Workflows for Future Intelligent Software is to enable anyone interested and prepared to study to explore the realm of artificial intelligence. Complex mathematics, new terms, and rapidly evolving technologies can be intimidating to many novices. By dividing ideas into digestible chunks and using straightforward language and useful examples that instill confidence right away, this book breaks down that barrier.

Readers will progress through these pages from the fundamentals of Python programming to critical data management skills and fundamental mathematical concepts that underpin machine learning. Every chapter is organized to connect theory and practice, ensuring that explanations are promptly reinforced through guided workflows and small projects. The book uses real-world examples to demonstrate how intelligent systems are developed, trained, assessed, and enhanced rather than just offering abstract formulas.

By the end of this tutorial, readers will know how to think like a machine learning practitioner and build Python code for AI applications. This book equips novices to confidently take the first steps toward creating future intelligent software solutions in a changing digital world by emphasizing clarity, useful application, and responsible creation.

CHAPTER I

Python Programming Essentials

Python Environment Setup

An essential first step for anyone starting out in machine learning and artificial intelligence is setting up a Python environment. A stable and well-designed environment is essential for novices because it guarantees that all required tools, libraries, and dependencies function together effortlessly, reducing irritation and optimizing learning opportunities. Python's ease of use, readability, and vast ecosystem of libraries and frameworks tailored for data analysis, modeling, and neural network creation make it a favorite in AI and machine learning. Therefore, before beginning to code and experiment, it is crucial to learn how to set up a Python environment correctly.

Installing Python is the first step in creating a Python environment. Python comes in two primary versions: Python 2 and Python 3. Because of its continuous support and compatibility with the newest libraries, Python 3 is the version that is advised for AI and machine learning projects. Python installations for Windows, macOS, and Linux are available on the official Python website, where beginners can download the language. To enable the operating system to recognize Python commands in the terminal or command prompt, it is crucial to make sure that the installation process involves adding Python to the system path. This minor action streamlines the future script execution and package installation process. Distributions like Anaconda, which come preloaded with Python, package management tools, and a plethora of libraries frequently used in AI and machine learning, can be especially useful for individuals who prefer an all-in-one solution.

Installing a package management system is the next step after installing Python. Third-party libraries can be easily installed and managed by users using pip, Python's built-in package management. These libraries contain necessary tools like scikit-learn for machine learning methods, Matplotlib and Seaborn for data visualization, Pandas for data manipulation, and NumPy for numerical computation. Installing libraries with pip guarantees that the user has access to the most recent versions of these tools, and it is as easy as running a command in the terminal. Conda is a standalone package manager that manages several Python environments and handles library installations for novice Anaconda users. Because it enables users to separate project dependencies without creating conflicts, this is particularly helpful when working on various projects that could require different library versions.

Another crucial step in setting up Python for AI and machine learning is creating virtual environments. An isolated workspace with its own Python interpreter and library installations is called a virtual environment. Beginners can keep their working workspace tidy and avoid dependency conflicts between projects by utilizing virtual environments. Python's built-in venv module or Conda, if Anaconda is being used, can be used to construct virtual environments. The user can install project-specific libraries without changing the global Python installation by activating the virtual environment after it has been created. Since various projects may require different versions of TensorFlow, PyTorch, or other frameworks, this technique is particularly crucial in the fields of artificial intelligence and machine learning. Stability and repeatability throughout development workflows are guaranteed by the appropriate use of virtual environments.

Selecting an integrated development environment (IDE) or code editor is crucial after installing Python, libraries, and configuring virtual environments. Beginners typically find interactive and beginner-friendly IDEs like Jupyter Notebook incredibly beneficial because it allows code, visuals, and explanatory text to coexist in a single interface. Because Jupyter Notebook facilitates iterative experimentation, allowing users to test short code segments, display data, and instantly see results, it is especially well-liked in the fields of artificial intelligence and machine learning. More conventional programming environments with sophisticated capabilities like code completion, debugging, and version control integration are offered by other IDEs like Visual Studio Code or PyCharm. Although choosing an IDE is a matter of personal opinion, it is imperative that novices learn how to use these tools efficiently because they will greatly improve learning and productivity.

To make sure the environment works as intended, testing the setup is an essential first step. To import installed libraries and make sure they are configured correctly, beginners need to develop brief Python scripts. It is recommended to evaluate frameworks like TensorFlow or PyTorch for AI and machine learning by executing simple operations or sample models. Errors that arise during this phase frequently point to difficulties with environment path settings, library installation, or compatibility; fixing them early on in the development process helps avoid more complicated issues later on. This verification procedure gives the novice confidence in the setup and guarantees that there won't be any technical difficulties as they go.

Beginners should install Python and libraries and think about utilizing Git or other version control systems. Version control enables users to interact with others, keep track of code changes, and save project backups. Projects can be safely kept or shared in repositories hosted by platforms such as GitHub or GitLab. This approach is helpful for novices in AI and machine learning, not only for code management but also for keeping track of datasets, notebooks, and experiment logs. A professional workflow is guaranteed, and a solid basis for future cooperative projects is established by integrating version control with the Python environment and IDE.

Lastly, to preserve compatibility and gain access to new capabilities, it is essential to keep the Python environment updated. Bug fixes, speed enhancements, and new features that can benefit AI and machine learning applications are frequently included in library upgrades. While keeping in mind the limitations of the virtual environment, beginners should update Python, the package management, and individual libraries on a regular basis. Projects that receive regular updates stay operational while taking advantage of advancements in the Python ecosystem. Beginners may create a solid basis for studying AI and machine learning by keeping a well-configured, updated, and tested Python environment. This allows them to concentrate on experimenting with algorithms, evaluating data, and creating models rather than resolving technical problems.

For anyone new to the field of artificial intelligence and machine learning, a well-configured Python environment speeds up learning and lowers barriers. Every step helps create a stable and adaptable workplace, from setting up Python and managing libraries to setting up virtual environments, choosing an IDE, and implementing version control. Taking the time to set up the environment at the beginning properly not only prevents future problems but also encourages best practices that will be carried over into more complex projects. By methodically completing these setup procedures, students establish a polished and effective work environment that fosters investigation, testing, and development in the quickly developing fields of artificial intelligence and machine learning, setting the stage for a more thorough comprehension and real-world implementation of these game-changing technologies. By offering a clear path from initial setup to successful project execution, our organized method guarantees that novices spend more time honing their abilities and putting AI solutions into practice rather than debugging environmental obstacles.

Core Syntax Rules

For novices, especially those who want to investigate artificial intelligence and machine learning, it is essential to comprehend the fundamental syntactic principles of Python. Python is a great first programming language because of its well-known readability and simplicity of syntax. To determine the flow of a program, Python mostly uses indentation and short, straightforward statements, in contrast to other programming languages that demand a lot of punctuation and rigid structural restrictions. Because of its simplicity, novices can concentrate more on understanding programming principles rather than becoming bogged down by intricate syntax. Because Python defines code blocks rather than braces or keywords, indentation is especially important. For instance, appropriate indentation guarantees that the interpreter knows which lines of code correspond to which block in conditional statements, loops, and function definitions. Syntax problems, which are frequently among the first challenges for novice programmers, can result from neglecting indentation. Thus, understanding this fundamental principle is necessary before advancing to more intricate programming ideas in machine learning and artificial intelligence.

Python stores data in variables, and another fundamental component of syntax is the rules for naming variables. Letters, digits, or underscores must come after the initial letter or underscore in variable names. Since they are case-sensitive, "Data" and "data" are regarded as distinct variables. Because incorrect naming might result in unexpected behavior or problems in a program, it is essential to understand this distinction. Moreover, Python supports dynamic typing, which enables a variable to store several data types at various stages of the program. For example, a variable may be assigned to a string after first storing an integer. This adaptability facilitates quick experimentation, which is essential for understanding AI algorithms and machine learning models, and is practical for novices. However, when executing operations that anticipate a certain data type, dynamic typing also necessitates close attention to prevent type mistakes.

An integral component of Python's grammar rules, operators are symbols that carry out operations on variables and values. Python has comparison operators, including equality, inequality, greater than, and less than, in addition to the simple arithmetic operators of addition, subtraction, multiplication, and division. These operators are essential for building conditional expressions and managing program flow. More intricate decision-making is made possible by logical operators like "and," "or," and "not," which are frequently required in machine learning jobs where several circumstances need to be assessed. Additionally, beginners should comprehend augmented assignment operators, which combine assignment with bitwise or arithmetic operations, and assignment operators, which assign values to variables. Understanding operators is essential since they have a direct impact on how algorithms handle and modify data, which in turn affects how machine learning models behave.

Python's control flow constructs, such as loops and conditional statements, are subject to stringent grammar guidelines that novices must carefully adhere to. Programs can make judgments based on specific criteria by using conditional statements like "if," "elif," and "else." The indented piece of code underneath these statements indicates the action performed if the condition is met, and Python requires that these statements be followed by a colon. Iterating over data sets is a common activity in AI and machine learning, and loops like "for" and "while" are essential for repeating tasks. The repeating code must be appropriately indented, and each loop statement must conclude with a colon. Developing effective and accurate programs requires an understanding of control flow principles, particularly when putting into practice algorithms that handle massive volumes of data or carry out iterative optimization, which are frequent in machine learning.

Another essential element of Python syntax that allows for code modularity and reusability is functions. The "def" keyword, the function name, and any parentheses that may contain parameters are used to define functions. The "return" statement can be used to optionally return a value, and the function body needs to be indented. Functions make it simpler for novices to test and debug intricate AI operations by helping them arrange code logically. Additionally, they make code reuse easier, enabling students to utilize the same procedures on other data sets without having to redo the code. Since it is the foundation of practically every programming work, from data preprocessing to implementing machine learning algorithms, it is essential to comprehend the syntactic rules for defining and invoking functions. If the fundamental syntax rules are not completely grasped, incorrect function definitions—such as misaligned indentation or missing colons—can cause code to fail to execute and irritate novices.

Beginners must learn the special syntactic rules that Python uses for managing data structures. Common structures for storing data collections include lists, tuples, dictionaries, and sets. Both tuples and lists are ordered collections; tuples are immutable, while lists are mutable. According to syntax standards, the items of these structures must be surrounded in square brackets for lists or parentheses for tuples, and they must be separated by commas. Curly braces are necessary for dictionaries that hold key-value pairs, with a colon (:) separating each key and value. Curly brackets or the set() method are used to initialize sets, which stand for distinct elements. Since data structures are vital to effectively manipulating, storing, and retrieving data—a frequently required skill in AI projects—a thorough comprehension of these laws is imperative. Understanding these grammatical principles is essential for successful programming since inappropriate use of immutable structures, misplaced brackets, or wrong separators can result in errors or unexpected behavior.

Apart from these fundamental components, Python has particular guidelines for importing and utilizing libraries, which are particularly pertinent in the fields of artificial intelligence and machine learning. Libraries like scikit-learn, pandas, and numpy offer prebuilt classes and functions that speed up the creation of intricate algorithms. The "import" keyword is usually used in the syntax for importing modules, with the ability to choose import particular functions or classes or rename modules using "as." Runtime issues may result from code that is unable to access these libraries due to improper import syntax. Understanding these guidelines enables novices to efficiently utilize the extensive Python toolkit, cutting down on the time and effort needed to deploy AI and machine learning solutions. Adhering to correct syntax guarantees seamless integration of other modules and frees up novices to concentrate on the logic of their programs rather than fixing little mistakes.

Python error handling also adheres to specific syntax guidelines that are crucial for novices to comprehend. Try-except blocks are used in Python to handle and capture exceptions that might arise while a program is running. Code that may raise an exception is contained in the "try" block, and code to handle the exception in the event that it arises is contained in the "except" block. Because of this structure, programs are less likely to fail suddenly, and students can create strong algorithms that can manage a variety of data inputs and runtime irregularities. The syntax calls for appropriately indented blocks underneath the "try" and "except" declarations, followed by colons. In AI and machine learning, where data inconsistencies and computational errors are frequent and strong handling techniques are required to preserve program stability, it is particularly crucial to comprehend this error-handling vocabulary.

Additionally, Python has documentation and commenting guidelines that are essential for preserving code clarity and readability. While multi-line comments are surrounded by triple quotes, single-line comments start with the hash symbol. In addition to helping novices record their ideas, proper commenting promotes teamwork, which is essential in AI projects because several developers may be working on the same codebase. Following these grammar rules guarantees that code stays comprehensible and maintainable, which is a skill that gets more crucial as projects get more complicated. Debugging and iterative development, which are essential components of the machine learning workflow, are also made easier by code that is clear and well-documented.

Beginners of Python can concentrate on more complex ideas in artificial intelligence and machine learning by having a solid foundation in these fundamental grammar principles. Learners can write code that is both understandable and functional by becoming proficient in indentation, variable names, operators, control flow, functions, data structures, library usage, error handling, and commenting. Beginners can freely experiment with programming concepts thanks to this foundation, which also lessens irritation caused by typical syntax problems. These syntactic rules are continually applicable as learners progress, offering a solid foundation for building increasingly intricate AI models, machine learning pipelines, and data analysis activities. Understanding Python's fundamental grammar rules is a crucial first step for anyone starting a journey into artificial intelligence and machine learning. Python's simplicity and strength make it a perfect introductory language.

Variables and Data Structures

Anyone learning Python must have a basic understanding of variables and data structures, particularly when tackling machine learning and artificial intelligence. As named memory storage locations that store data values, variables are the fundamental building blocks of Python programming. They offer a means of storing, modifying, and retrieving data—a necessity for calculations, dataset analysis, and machine learning model training. Python is more versatile and beginner-friendly than some other programming languages since it does not require the explicit definition of variable types. Because of dynamic typing, variables can store various kinds of data, including text, numbers, and more complicated structures, and they can change type while the program is running if necessary. In AI and machine learning, where data frequently originates in a variety of formats and may require transformation or preprocessing before being employed in models, this flexibility is especially helpful.

Variables in Python can store a variety of data types. Numerical kinds include floating-point numbers, which represent decimal values, and integers, which represent whole numbers. For computations involving weights, biases, and statistical operations, these are crucial in machine learning. Another popular data type is strings, which are essential for managing textual data like filenames, labels, and raw input data. Strings are collections of characters. Additionally essential are boolean values, which can be either true or false, particularly in conditional statements, logic operations, and code decision-making procedures. Beginners can concentrate on comprehending algorithms and data manipulation instead of being constrained by intricate syntax or stringent type restrictions, thanks to Python's ability to handle these fundamental data types with ease.

Python offers a wide range of data structures in addition to basic variables for effective data management and organization. One of Python's most flexible data structures, lists are ordered collections of elements that can be altered after they are created. Lists are very flexible since they can contain elements of many sorts, such as texts, numbers, or even other lists. Python has many built-in methods for manipulating lists, including adding, deleting, and sorting members. They are frequently used to store data sequences, such as feature vectors, datasets, or model predictions. Similar to lists, tuples are immutable, which means that once defined, their content cannot be altered. Because of their immutability, tuples can be used to represent fixed data sets, like coordinates, configuration parameters, or other variables that must not change while a program is running.

Another strong Python data structure is a dictionary, which provides a means of storing key-value pairs. As opposed to lists, which rely on sequential placement, this enables quick data retrieval based on unique identifiers. In AI and machine learning, dictionaries are especially helpful for storing mappings, including label-to-class relationships, configuration settings, or outcomes linked to certain keys. Another type of data structure is a set, which is an unordered collection of distinct elements. They are useful for removing duplicate data or for membership testing, including filtering unique values from input data or distinguishing different categories in a dataset. Beginners can efficiently manage data by knowing when and how to use each data structure, which guarantees efficient memory utilization and faster computation in machine learning processes.

Python data structures are not just flexible but also intricately linked with the syntax and functionality of the language. When working with multidimensional datasets, the ability to index and slice lists and tuples is essential for providing access to particular elements or sub-sequences. Dictionaries make it easier to organize complex data by supporting simple key-based operations for adding, changing, and retrieving values. For tasks like feature selection, data preparation, and cleaning, sets offer built-in operations like union, intersection, and difference. In AI and machine learning projects, where data processing is sometimes the most crucial and time-consuming step, these features enable novices to work with data using little code while preserving readability and clarity.

Through additional libraries, Python can also handle sophisticated data structures, which are particularly useful in machine learning and artificial intelligence. For instance, the array is presented by NumPy as a high-performance data structure designed for numerical calculations. Arrays greatly increase efficiency by enabling actions on vast datasets without the need for explicit loops. When working with big input feature matrices, neural network weight matrices, or machine learning model outputs, this vectorized method is crucial. DataFrames, two-dimensional labeled data structures that combine the versatility of dictionaries and the effectiveness of arrays, are provided by Pandas, another popular package. DataFrames, which offer capabilities for indexing, filtering, aggregating, and manipulating data, make it easy for novices to work with tabular data. Gaining proficiency with these extended data formats is a prerequisite for successfully applying machine learning techniques.

Knowing scope and memory management is crucial when working with variables and data structures in Python. The scope of variables might be local, global, or nonlocal, which affects how and where they can be accessed and changed. Cleaner code is encouraged, data integrity is guaranteed, and accidental overwrites are avoided with proper variable scope management. It's critical to distinguish between operations that produce copies and references because data structures, particularly huge lists or arrays, can use a lot of memory. For example, there may be differences in the effects on memory use and program behavior between making changes to an existing list and starting from scratch. When working with huge datasets, which are typical in machine learning, where accuracy and efficiency are crucial, these factors become crucial.

Performing operations and data transformations is another aspect of working with variables and data structures. The arithmetic, comparison, and logical operators that Python offers for basic variables are essential for developing algorithms and putting mathematical models into practice. Beginners can turn raw data into representations appropriate for machine learning by transforming, aggregating, and iterating over data structures. Code is easier to maintain and debug when complex processes are carried out succinctly and readablely using list comprehensions, dictionary comprehensions, and generator expressions. These methods enable novices to do preprocessing tasks that are essential for training successful machine learning models, such as feature extraction, normalization, and categorical variable encoding.

Another essential component of learning Python for AI and machine learning is debugging and testing variables and data structures. Inspecting variable types, examining contents, and confirming that data structures operate as intended should all become second nature to beginners. Easy commands to analyze lengths, check types, or print numbers give quick feedback and boost confidence in data comprehension. In later phases of machine learning workflows, where inaccurate assumptions about data formats or content might result in subpar model performance, this hands-on approach helps avoid mistakes. Beginners may effectively manipulate and manage data by having a solid understanding of variables and data structures early on. This builds the foundation for more complex ideas like algorithm implementation, model training, and performance evaluation.

In conclusion, studying variables and data structures is a crucial first step for Python newbies, especially those who want to work in machine learning and artificial intelligence. While Python's flexible data structures give strong tools for organizing, retrieving, and altering information, variables offer the fundamental way of storing and manipulating data. Every structure, from basic dictionaries and lists to sophisticated arrays and DataFrames, has a distinct function and facilitates effective processing. In addition to facilitating efficient coding, knowing how to choose, modify, and handle various data constructions improves problem-solving abilities and gets novices ready for the intricate data difficulties that arise in AI and machine learning projects. Gaining expertise in these areas lays the groundwork for future research and success in this quickly changing profession by ensuring that students are prepared to handle the variety of data kinds and structures they will come across.

Functions and Code Organization

Python's core ideas of functions and code organization serve as the foundation for creating effective, understandable, and manageable programs—especially for novices interested in machine learning and artificial intelligence. Programmers can use functions to condense a collection of instructions into a reusable block of code that can be called repeatedly without requiring the logic to be rewritten throughout a program. Because faults can be isolated to specific methods rather than spreading throughout a vast codebase, this modular approach not only makes code cleaner and shorter, but it also makes debugging and testing easier. Functions offer an organized method for regularly carrying out repetitive activities like data preprocessing, feature extraction, or model evaluation, which are frequently a part of algorithms in the context of artificial intelligence and machine learning. Early function design experiments allow beginners to learn how to pass input data, carry out operations, and return output while keeping their code clear.

The def keyword, a function name, parentheses (which may contain parameters), and a colon are required when defining a function in Python. The body of the function, which contains the instructions to be carried out, is the indented block that appears beneath this line. Functions can receive input data thanks to parameters, which gives them flexibility and situational adaptability. While not all functions must return a value, the return statement is used to convey output back to the section of the program that invoked the function. Because poorly specified or disorganized functions might result in unexpected behavior or runtime errors, it is essential to understand how to define and use functions correctly. It is crucial to understand these guidelines early in a learner's journey because novices frequently make mistakes like forgetting indentation, using incorrect variable names for parameters, or misinterpreting the scope of variables inside and outside functions.

Because they encourage code reuse and eliminate redundancy, functions are particularly essential for organizing larger programs. For example, functions for tasks like normalizing datasets, dividing data into training and testing groups, or computing accuracy measures are frequently implemented in AI projects. A newbie can call a single function for every task without having to repeat the same code, which ensures consistency and lowers the possibility of errors. Additionally, this method makes the code easier to read, making it possible for someone else to evaluate it or even the coder to revisit it weeks later to comprehend its structure and intent rapidly. Well-structured Python programs are built on the foundation of clear function names and succinct code inside each function, which makes it simpler to add or change functionality as AI or machine learning tasks get more complicated.

Python promotes grouping code into modules and packages in addition to individual functions, which enhances readability and maintainability even more. A module is a Python code file that can be imported into other scripts using the import statement. It is often made up of functions, classes, and variables. This reduces clutter in the main script by enabling programmers to divide conceptually distinct portions of their software into separate files. Even larger projects can be neatly structured with packages, which are collections of modules arranged into directories with a certain structure. Because machine learning workflows usually entail numerous steps, including data collecting, preprocessing, feature engineering, model training, and evaluation, modular code organization is frequently advantageous for novices working on AI projects. Code management is made easier by breaking these steps down into distinct modules and functions, which also allows students to concentrate on a single step at a time without feeling overburdened by the pipeline as a whole.

The idea of variable scope, which determines where a variable can be accessed within a program, is another crucial component of code organization. Unless specifically returned or designated as global, variables defined inside a function are local to that function and cannot be accessed outside of it. This scope method lowers the possibility of overwriting crucial data and helps avoid unexpected interactions between various program components. Since AI systems frequently comprise numerous functions managing shared datasets or model parameters, it is crucial for newcomers to understand the difference between local and global variables. Careful function design and code organization are crucial since mismanaging variable scope can result in subtle errors that are hard to find.

Additionally, anonymous functions—also referred to as lambda functions—are supported by Python and offer a condensed method of defining brief, one-time functions without giving them names. Lambda functions are very helpful for tasks like defining a key function for sorting or applying a transformation to every member in a list.

Lambda functions may be puzzling to novices at first, but when used in conjunction with other functions like map, filter, and reduce, they become an effective tool for writing clear, understandable code in AI processes. More elegant solutions to data manipulation problems that are frequently encountered in machine learning are made possible by the proper usage of lambda functions in conjunction with well-structured named functions.

An essential part of function and code organization is documentation and comments. It is easier for others to understand how to use a function when you write clear docstrings inside of it that explain its purpose, inputs, and outputs. Well-documented functions enable learners and collaborators to rapidly understand the logic and purpose of each component in AI projects, which frequently involve difficult mathematical operations or data transformations. When followed, the rules for naming functions, structuring code, and crafting understandable comments provided by Python's PEP 8 style guide improve both individual learning and professional coding practices. By forming these practices early on, novices may make sure that their code is not only functional but also comprehensible, maintainable, and scalable as projects get bigger and more complicated.

Well-structured functions also make testing and debugging easier. Only when functions are modular and self-contained can unit testing—which tests individual functions separately—be carried out. In AI and machine learning, where inaccurate computations or data handling can have a substantial impact on model performance, this method is very advantageous. Beginners can find issues more quickly and fix them without impacting unrelated portions of the code by breaking the program down into testable functions. Additionally, iterative development is supported by structured code organization, which enables students to improve their algorithms, try out various strategies, and incorporate new features without interfering with the workflow as a whole.

Python promotes object-oriented programming in addition to functions, which improves code structure even more. Classes enable the grouping of functions and data into coherent units that represent concepts or objects in a program. Classes' methods, which are linked to particular objects and perform similarly to functions, provide for a more structured and scalable program design. Classes in AI and machine learning can stand in for pipelines, models, or datasets, offering an organized foundation for putting intricate procedures into practice. Combining functions and object-oriented concepts gives novices a deeper understanding of program architecture, which facilitates the efficient management of complex AI projects.

Lastly, the act of structuring code into classes, modules, and functions promotes sound programming practices, which are essential for sustained success in machine learning and artificial intelligence. It promotes clarity, modular design, and logical thinking—all of which are critical when dealing with complex algorithms and huge datasets. Early adoption of these concepts prepares beginners to handle more sophisticated subjects like computer vision, deep learning, and natural language processing without being intimidated by the complexity of the code. Learners may create reliable, maintainable, and effective Python programs that provide a strong basis for investigating the more general domains of artificial intelligence and machine learning by giving functions and code organization first priority.

Importing and Using Libraries

Libraries in Python are essential for increasing the language's functionality and enabling both novice and expert programmers to carry out intricate tasks with less code. In essence, a library is a collection of pre-written code that offers particular capabilities, such as machine learning, statistical analysis, data visualization, and numerical computations. Python programmers can benefit from the knowledge of a large community, avoid making the same mistakes twice, and concentrate on problem-solving instead of creating fundamental tools from scratch by importing and utilizing libraries. Because algorithms and processes in artificial intelligence and machine learning can be quite complicated and call for reliable, optimized implementations, this skill is especially crucial. In order to access powerful tools and maintain well-structured, effective code, beginners must first learn how to import and use libraries correctly.

Python offers a straightforward yet adaptable library import system. A library's functions and classes are made usable by bringing it into the current workspace using the import statement. Depending on the demands of the programmer, there are multiple ways to import libraries. Importing the complete library is a popular method that gives access to all of its modules, methods, and classes. This is frequently accomplished by prefixing each function call with the name of the library. For instance, using functions for square roots, trigonometry, or exponential computations is made possible by importing a mathematics library. This approach lessens the possibility of name conflicts by clearly stating the provenance of each function, which helps to maintain code clarity. This clarity helps newcomers understand how various library functions work and interact with one another.

Python lets you import specific methods or classes from a library in addition to whole libraries. When only a portion of a library's functionality is required, this approach works well. Beginners can avoid needless costs and develop clearer, more concise code by importing specific components. Aliasing, which gives a library or function a shorter name for convenience, is another feature that Python enables. Function calls can become frequent and lengthy in libraries used extensively in AI and machine learning, such as data processing frameworks or libraries for numerical computation. When aliases are used correctly, coding becomes easier without sacrificing readability, allowing novices to concentrate on comprehending algorithm logic rather than tedious syntax.

Many of the modules in Python's standard library offer built-in functionality without the need for additional installations. These consist of modules for handling files, manipulating dates and times, creating random numbers, mathematics, and operating system interactions. The standard library is a useful tool for novices to learn how to organize programs and carry out routine operations effectively. These built-in libraries act as a springboard to more sophisticated third-party libraries and promote a fundamental understanding of Python's capabilities. For tasks like data preparation, creating random datasets, and conducting preliminary investigations of structured or unstructured data, standard libraries are especially helpful in machine learning.

Python's capabilities are further expanded by third-party libraries, especially in the fields of machine learning and artificial intelligence. Beginners can easily deal with arrays, matrices, and big datasets thanks to libraries like NumPy, which offer incredibly efficient data structures and operations for numerical computations. Pandas provides structured dataset data manipulation capabilities that enable data transformation, grouping, and filtering in advance of model training. Understanding trends and patterns in data requires the ability to produce plots, charts, and graphs in an intuitive manner, which is made possible by visualization frameworks like Matplotlib and Seaborn. Libraries dedicated to machine learning, such as scikit-learn, TensorFlow, and PyTorch, provide pre-built frameworks and algorithms for model training, performance analysis, and the implementation of prediction solutions. Beginners can access sophisticated functionality without having to start from scratch by importing and using these libraries, which speeds up their learning and project development.

Package management systems make it easier to install and maintain third-party libraries. Installing, updating, and removing libraries using straightforward commands is made possible by Pip, Python's default package management. It is simple for novices to experiment with new tools and frameworks because installing libraries only requires one line of code. Similar capabilities and environment management are provided by the conda package manager for users of distributions like Anaconda, which is especially helpful for keeping distinct configurations for various projects. All dependencies are satisfied when libraries are managed properly, which minimizes conflicts and improves reproducibility. To ensure consistency when sharing projects or transferring code between computers, beginners should make it a habit to record library versions and installations.

The idea of modular programming is closely related to library imports. Libraries provide well-defined modules that contain functionality that may be imported and used again in different projects. This modular strategy lowers redundancy, increases maintainability, and encourages code reuse. This structure helps beginners grasp how functions, classes, and methods interact as well as how to arrange code into logical pieces. In-depth examples and documentation are also provided by many libraries, enabling users to investigate capabilities methodically. Beginners can learn best practices, hone their problem-solving abilities, and build confidence when applying sophisticated techniques to real-world datasets by reading documentation and playing with library functions.

Knowing dependencies and compatibility is another crucial component of using libraries in Python. Versions of libraries may make modifications or deprecate particular functionality, and some libraries depend on other packages to work properly. Novices should know how to securely update libraries, fix dependency problems, and verify library versions. Here, virtual environments are essential because they make it possible to isolate library installations for certain tasks. Beginners may guarantee that modifications to one project's library configuration do not affect others, preserving stability and repeatability, by setting up a specific environment for each project. In AI and machine learning, where models may depend on exact versions of libraries to generate reliable results, this technique is particularly crucial.

The practical features of importing and using libraries, such as investigating accessible functions, comprehending parameters, and incorporating library functions into workflows, should also become second nature to beginners. Because they let users experiment with code snippets, display outputs, and iterate improve their usage of libraries, interactive environments like Jupyter Notebook are especially beneficial. Importing a plotting library and experimenting with its visualization features on sample data, for instance, offers practical experience and increases comprehension. Similar to this, novices can better understand ideas like feature selection, model training, and evaluation by importing a machine learning library and playing with small datasets. This hands-on method speeds up learning and increases self-assurance while using libraries for more challenging tasks.

In summary, importing and utilizing libraries is a crucial ability for Python novices, especially those experimenting with AI and machine learning. Libraries offer pre-built functionality and tools that let users access sophisticated algorithms, complete complicated tasks quickly, and concentrate on problem-solving rather than low-level implementation. Beginners may write clear, well-structured code by learning how to import whole libraries, use aliases efficiently, and import particular functions. A reliable and repeatable workflow is ensured by managing installations, dependencies, and environments in addition to comprehending the function of standard and third-party libraries. In addition to improving a beginner's programming skills, mastering these techniques paves the way for fruitful experimentation, model building, and real-world application in the quickly developing domains of artificial intelligence and machine learning. A solid understanding of library usage enables novices to take advantage of Python's full potential, promoting a more seamless transition from learning fundamental ideas to putting real-world solutions into practice.

From Syntax to Self-Reliance

This chapter is important because it turns programming from a theoretical concept into a set of useful skills that you can use right now. Writing code that executes is only one aspect of learning how to configure your environment, comprehend basic grammar, organize functions, structure data, and import libraries. It's about laying the groundwork that will define how empowering or irritating your future Python work will feel. When these fundamentals are successfully implemented, work goes more smoothly, faults are easier to identify, and each script you finish boosts your confidence. But when they are disregarded, minor errors add up to confusion, jumbled code becomes challenging to debug, and development drastically slows down. Cleaner automation at work, quicker data analysis, improved teamwork, and the capacity to transform concepts into useful tools without total reliance on others are just a few examples of how the difference manifests itself in real life.

You start thinking like a programmer instead of just duplicating commands when you put what you've learned in this chapter into practice. Technical friction is decreased as your environment becomes dependable and consistent. Your proficiency with syntax keeps trivial mistakes from impeding your productivity. Real-world problems can be properly modeled with the use of structured variables and data collecting. Programs with well-designed functions are scalable and reusable. When libraries are used properly, they give you access to a worldwide ecosystem of tools that significantly increase your capabilities. These modifications are not hypothetical. They have an impact on how rapidly you can develop revenue-generating applications, automate tedious operations, analyze data, and prototype ideas.

The repercussions of disregarding these principles are subtle but severe. Code that is disorganized is difficult to maintain. Misunderstandings arise from irregular formatting and poor naming, particularly in collaborative settings. Programs that lack structured functions turn into lengthy, convoluted scripts that are prone to breaking. Inadequate library management can result in version conflicts or hard-to-trace mistakes. This discouragement may cause students to think that programming is hard by nature, while in fact, the problem is rooted in shaky foundations. Ignoring these fundamentals can have real-world consequences, such as slowed initiatives, lost opportunities, and wasted effort fixing avoidable errors.

Think about a real-world example. Let's say you wish to create a simple budgeting application that determines monthly savings and expenses. Installing required libraries, including those for managing spreadsheets, is possible with a Python environment that is appropriately set up. You can store revenue, expenses, and categories in structured data types like dictionaries or lists by using proper syntax and well-organized variables. To compute totals and percentages, you construct reusable functions.

In order to export the results into a structured report, you must import a library last. With repeatable accuracy, tasks that once required days of human spreadsheet manipulation can now be finished in a matter of seconds. This is the distinction between learning Python on the surface and being proficient in its fundamentals.

This is aptly illustrated in a short narrative. Once, a student tried automating the grading process for a tiny tutoring company. She initially produced a single, lengthy script with inconsistent variable names and repeated code blocks. For a while, it worked, but the script broke in several places when she needed to modify the grading formula. Exasperated, she went over the basics again. She segregated logic from input and output processes, standardized her naming conventions, and restructured her code into distinct functions. She just had to change one function the next time she needed to update the grading regulations, and the system as a whole adjusted right away. Her appreciation for basic structure, rather than her intelligence, was what changed.

Consider this chapter to be like building a house's foundation. The measurements that keep walls straight are called syntax rules. Everything else is supported via variables and data structures. The rooms that effectively arrange space are called functions. Libraries serve as the communication, water, and energy conduits that link your home to the outside world. No amount of ornamentation will stabilize a structure with an uneven base. However, you may boldly grow once the foundation is solid.

Use the CLEAR Code Framework: Configure, Lay Out, Extract, Apply, Review to put what you've learned into practice right now. Set up your environment correctly first. Make sure your editor is configured, that Python is installed appropriately, and that any dependencies are managed using virtual environments. Second, before writing a lot of logic, lay out your problem by choosing suitable data structures and establishing variables. Third, keep your code modular by separating repetitive logic into functions. Fourth, strategically use libraries rather than inventing pre-existing solutions. Lastly, check and rework your code to make it more efficient, readable, and clear. Every time you begin a new Python project, no matter how tiny, you can follow these five steps.

You will be able to create and oversee a dependable Python development environment that facilitates effective coding at the end of this chapter. You will be able to construct Python programs that adhere to consistent structural principles and are syntactically accurate by the end of this chapter. You will be able to create programs with proper variables, data structures, and modular functions for reuse and clarity by the end of this chapter. You will be able to use external libraries to expand your program's capability beyond the fundamentals by the end of this chapter. You will be able to restructure basic scripts into structured, maintainable code that can be used for practical tasks at the end of this chapter.

Consider for a moment how you will apply these foundations in the future. What routine task in your personal or professional life could a simple Python script automate? To what extent do you feel comfortable establishing a hygienic development environment on your own? Do you give readability the same priority as functionality while you're examining your code? In what situations have you previously been frustrated when a more robust organization may have avoided the situation? How are you going to make sure that every new script you write adheres to the same structure? Which library, if you deliberately looked into it, could improve your next project right away? What potential effects might better code organization have on teamwork?

This chapter's real value is in developing disciplined habits that build up over time, not in learning orders by heart.

Being proficient in the fundamentals does more than make you a better programmer. It equips you with the ability to analyze methodically, solve issues quickly, and create tools that have quantifiable effects in practical situations.

CHAPTER II

Data Handling and Preparation

Types of Data in AI

Artificial intelligence and machine learning are based on data, and for novice Python users, knowing the different kinds of data is essential. The design of algorithms, the training of models, and the interpretation of predictions are all impacted by the types of data. Numerical, categorical, textual, time-series, image, and multimedia data are the general categories into which Python data may be divided. Each of these types of data has unique properties, difficulties, and AI applications. Numbers make up numerical data, which can be continuous or discrete. Countable values, like the quantity of clients, transactions, or objects in a picture, are examples of discrete data. Contrarily, continuous data, which includes measures like temperature, height, weight, and sensor readings, can have any value within a range. Many AI models, especially those based on regression, clustering, or neural networks, rely heavily on numerical input because statistical analysis and mathematical operations are directly applicable. To guarantee that models yield accurate results, beginners must understand how to manage numerical data, including methods for normalization, standardization, and handling missing or outlier values.

Unlike continuous values, categorical data represent discrete groupings or labels. Colors, product categories, user preferences, and medical diagnoses are a few examples. There are two types of categorical data: ordinal, where the categories have a particular ranking or order, and nominal, where the order of the categories is irrelevant. In Python, handling categorical data usually entails turning it into numerical representations for processing by machine learning techniques. Typical methods include label encoding, in which categories are given integer values, and one-hot encoding, in which each category is represented as a binary vector. Beginners must comprehend these conversions because incorrect handling might skew predictions or affect model performance. In classification issues, such as spam identification, sentiment analysis, or customer segmentation in AI applications, where the objective is to predict a category or class for a given input, categorical data is frequently utilized.

Another crucial kind of data in AI, especially for natural language processing, is textual data. Simple keywords, complete documents, chat conversations, social media posts, and news stories are all examples of text data. Processing textual data in Python includes methods for tokenization, stop word and punctuation removal, text conversion to lowercase, and word embeddings, TF-IDF, and bag-of-words conversion into numerical representations. Because textual data is unstructured, extremely changeable, and context-dependent, it poses special issues. Before submitting text to AI models, beginners should learn how to clean and preprocess it because poor preparation can lower the accuracy of tasks like topic modeling, language translation, and sentiment categorization. Beginners may easily create complex AI models thanks to Python modules like NLTK, spaCy, and Hugging Face, which offer strong capabilities for interacting with textual data.

Sequentially recorded data over time, such as stock prices, weather readings, sensor readings, or website traffic, is known as time-series data. One of the most important characteristics of time-series data for modeling and prediction is its temporal order. Time-series analysis in AI frequently entails projecting future values from past trends. Python offers tools for manipulating, analyzing, and visualizing time-series data, such as pandas and statsmodels, which aid in the comprehension of trends, seasonality, and anomalies. In order to stabilize trends, novices need to understand how to handle missing timestamps, organize time-series data, and use methods like differencing or rolling averages. Additionally, time-series knowledge is crucial for applications like demand forecasting, financial projections, and IoT sensor monitoring since machine learning frequently uses recurrent neural networks and long short-term memory models to handle sequential data.

Multimedia and image data are becoming more and more significant in AI, particularly in computer vision. Pixels are grouped in grids to form images, and each pixel may contain color information denoted by numerical values. Waveform samples or spectrograms can be used to represent audio data, while video data adds a temporal dimension. Python packages like OpenCV, PIL, and TensorFlow are frequently needed for processing multimedia data. To enhance model generalization, novices need to know how to normalize pixel values, transform photos to arrays, and enrich data. Medical image analysis, autonomous driving, facial recognition, and object detection are examples of AI applications that use picture and multimedia data. To guarantee that machine learning models produce reliable results, handling such data necessitates meticulous preprocessing and knowledge of formats, resolutions, and color channels.

Classifying both organized and unstructured data is crucial when using AI. Organized data that is kept in databases, spreadsheets, or tables, with each column denoting a feature and each row denoting a record, is referred to as structured data. This kind of data is compatible with conventional machine learning methods and is simple to evaluate. Text, pictures, music, and video, on the other hand, are examples of unstructured data since they don't have a set format. More intricate preprocessing is needed for unstructured data, and deep learning methods are frequently used for analysis. Beginners need to be able to differentiate between these kinds and select the best techniques for working with and evaluating them. While unstructured data frequently benefits from transformer models for text or convolutional neural networks for images, structured data is best suited for linear models, decision trees, and clustering.

In order to organize and manipulate AI datasets, Python additionally provides composite data types, including lists, dictionaries, and arrays. Sequences of data, which might be textual, numeric, or even nested collections, can be stored using lists and arrays. Key-value pairs, which are helpful for mapping and categorizing data in classification tasks, are kept in dictionaries. Since these data structures serve as the fundamental building blocks for supplying data to machine learning models, it is imperative that novices understand how to interact with them. Effective methods for handling tabular data, performing vectorized operations, and manipulating big datasets are offered by libraries like NumPy and pandas. When performing batch processing, applying transformations, or preparing training data for model training, this understanding is crucial.

Beginners need to understand the basic differences between feature data and labels in AI datasets. Labels stand for the target variable that the model seeks to predict, whereas features are the input factors that are utilized to forecast an outcome. While unsupervised learning uses only features to find patterns or clusters, supervised learning usually arranges data in pairs of features and labels. For model training, novices need to learn how to properly segregate features and labels, normalize feature values, and encode category labels. If this distinction is not handled correctly, the model may perform poorly, or the results may be misinterpreted. To ensure that models are appropriately assessed and generalize effectively to new data, Python offers capabilities for dividing datasets into training and testing sets.

Working with various data kinds also heavily relies on preparation and data quality. Important preprocessing procedures that have a direct impact on model performance include handling missing values, identifying outliers, normalizing distributions, and encoding categorical variables. To get data ready for AI algorithms, beginners need to know how to use these preprocessing methods in Python. These tasks are made easier by libraries like pandas, scikit-learn, and NumPy, which offer functions for categorical data transformation, numerical data scaling, and missing value imputing. The data input into AI models is guaranteed to be clean, consistent, and appropriate for efficiently learning patterns when proper preprocessing is done.

In conclusion, for novices to use Python for machine learning and artificial intelligence projects successfully, they must have a solid understanding of the many kinds of data used in AI. Each type of data—numerical, category, textual, time-series, picture, or multimedia—has distinct properties and needs a particular method of handling. Preparing datasets requires the ability to distinguish between structured and unstructured data, organize data using composite structures, and distinguish features from labels. Model accuracy and dependability are further guaranteed by preprocessing and data quality control. By grasping these ideas, novices create a solid basis for putting AI algorithms into practice, creating machine learning models, and effectively using Python to solve real-world issues.

NumPy Array Operations

The Numerical Python library, or NumPy for short, is one of the most important resources for novices studying AI and machine learning because of its robust array features and fast numerical calculations. The array object, which offers a versatile and effective means of storing and manipulating numerical data, is the foundation of NumPy. NumPy arrays are homogenous, which means that every element must be of the same type, in contrast to Python's built-in lists. This enables optimum memory usage and efficiency. Because it allows for vectorized computations that are far faster than conventional Python loops, this homogeneity is especially useful for carrying out large-scale numerical operations. For novices, handling datasets effectively, carrying out mathematical transformations, and putting machine learning algorithms into practice all depend on a mastery of NumPy arrays and associated operations.

The first step in using NumPy is to create and initialize arrays. Python lists and tuples that already exist or functions that produce numerical sequences can be used to create arrays. For example, novices can represent vectors with one-dimensional arrays, matrices with two-dimensional arrays, or even more sophisticated data structures with higher-dimensional arrays. Additionally, NumPy has functions for creating arrays with certain characteristics, like arrays made up of ones, zeros, or random numbers selected from predetermined distributions. In machine learning, these initialization techniques are especially helpful for creating synthetic datasets for algorithm testing, initializing model parameters, and setting up weight matrices. The foundation for comprehending more complex AI and data processing activities is laid by the ability to precisely generate and manipulate arrays.

The ability of NumPy arrays to allow vectorized operations is among their most potent features. Vectorization removes the requirement for explicit loops by enabling mathematical operations to be carried out concurrently across all of an array's elements. When working with huge datasets, which are prevalent in AI applications, this functionality not only makes code simpler but also significantly increases computing performance. In addition to more complicated operations like exponentiation, logarithms, and trigonometric functions, beginners may execute arithmetic operations like addition, subtraction, multiplication, and division on large arrays simultaneously. For tasks like feature scaling, data normalization, and other preprocessing procedures needed in machine learning pipelines, the capacity to execute batch operations is crucial.

Broadcasting is another feature that NumPy arrays have, which enables compatible operations on arrays of various shapes. In order to facilitate element-wise operations without requiring manual reshaping, broadcasting automatically enlarges the smaller array to match the larger array's dimensions. Because it eliminates the need for repetitive code and enables more succinct and understandable processes, broadcasting is crucial for novices. For instance, it is possible to add a vector to every row of a matrix or a scalar value to an entire array without the need for explicit loops. In AI and machine learning processes, this functionality makes data transformations easier, boosts productivity, and offers a natural approach to applying operations across datasets.

Basic operations like indexing and slicing let novices access, alter, and work with particular NumPy array items or subsets. In order to access elements from the end of one-dimensional arrays, they can be indexed using either negative or integer positions. Row and column indexing, slicing, and even more complex indexing with boolean masks or integer arrays are supported by multi-dimensional arrays. When it comes to filtering data according to circumstances, like choosing just positive values, values above a threshold, or rows that satisfy specified requirements, boolean indexing is especially effective. These procedures are necessary for feature selection, data preparation, and cleaning—all crucial stages in getting datasets ready for machine learning models. Beginners may effectively manipulate and experiment with their data by learning indexing and slicing, which gives them exact control over their data.

Numerous statistical and aggregation techniques are also supported by NumPy arrays, which are essential for data analysis in AI and machine learning. Beginners may easily summarize datasets and learn about their features with functions like sum, mean, median, standard deviation, and variance. In multi-dimensional arrays, these aggregation algorithms can be used along particular axes, such as adding up rows or columns, or they can be used throughout the entire array. Tasks like normalization, outlier detection, and exploratory data analysis are made easier by this flexibility, which permits thorough examination of the features and labels in a dataset.

Beginners can gain a feel for patterns and distributions in the data by being able to execute these operations efficiently on huge arrays. This is crucial for creating machine learning models that work.

Arrays must also be reshaped, stacked, and split, among other crucial actions. When preparing data for machine learning algorithms that demand particular input shapes, reshaping enables arrays to be transformed into other dimensions without changing the underlying data. Multiple arrays can be combined into a single array using stacking techniques, such as vertical and horizontal stacking, which is helpful for combining features or datasets. On the other hand, arrays can be broken up into smaller parts using splitting operations for purposes like parallel computation, cross-validation, and batch processing. Gaining proficiency in these structural manipulations guarantees that novices can effectively arrange and preprocess data, which is an essential step in putting AI and machine learning workflows into practice.

For applications involving AI and machine learning, linear algebra operations on NumPy arrays are especially important. Numerous machine learning techniques, including regression, classification, and neural networks, rely on dot products, matrix multiplication, transposition, determinants, and eigenvalue computations, all of which NumPy supports. Gaining an understanding of these processes enables novices to manually apply fundamental algorithms, offering a more profound understanding of how models learn from data. For example, vector operations are widely employed in optimization techniques, while matrix multiplication is essential to neural networks' forward and backward propagation. Beginners can better utilize prebuilt machine learning frameworks and understand the mathematical underpinnings of AI models by becoming proficient in these array operations.

NumPy arrays are useful for mathematical and structural operations, as well as for random number generation in sampling, stochastic processes, and simulations. Beginners can use random number functions to accomplish random sampling, create reproducible datasets, and add stochastic components to algorithms. These features are especially helpful for testing models, assessing performance, and putting machine learning algorithms—like k-means clustering or neural network weight initialization—that depend on random initialization into practice. Beginners can test out various scenarios and obtain practical experience managing and altering data for AI applications by combining random operations with array manipulations.

To sum up, learning NumPy array operations is a prerequisite for Python novices who want to investigate machine learning and artificial intelligence. Vectorization, broadcasting, indexing, and aggregation allow for powerful and succinct operations on big datasets, while arrays offer an organized and effective means of storing, manipulating, and analyzing numerical data. Data processing and organization skills are further improved by reshaping, stacking, splitting, and linear algebra procedures, which get data ready for machine learning models. Understanding of stochastic and deterministic processes is strengthened by experimentation and testing made possible by random number generation and other specialized activities. Gaining expertise in these processes gives novices the tools they need for data analysis, preprocessing, and algorithm implementation, laying a solid basis for future research and success in AI and machine learning. In the quickly developing field of artificial intelligence, mastery of NumPy array operations not only simplifies coding and processing but also fosters a better comprehension of how data is represented and processed, bridging the gap between theory and real-world application.

Pandas DataFrames Basics

An indispensable tool for novices pursuing artificial intelligence and machine learning, Pandas is one of the most popular Python libraries for data analysis and manipulation. The DataFrame, a two-dimensional data structure at the heart of pandas, enables users to store and handle data in a tabular format, much like a spreadsheet or SQL table. DataFrames are perfect for preparing and studying datasets prior to applying AI algorithms because of their great flexibility and ability to handle a wide range of data kinds, including textual, numerical, and categorical data. Since effective data management, cleansing, and transformation are essential components of any machine learning workflow, it is imperative that novices grasp the fundamentals of DataFrames.

Depending on where the data comes from, there are several ways to create a DataFrame in Pandas. Using pandas built-in functions, novices can generate DataFrames from dictionaries, where keys stand for column names and values are lists of data, from lists of lists, or from pre-existing CSV, Excel, or SQL files. Users can easily switch from raw data files to structured DataFrames that are appropriate for analysis because of this flexibility. Row labels are called the index, while column labels are called headers. Each DataFrame is made up of rows and columns. Customizing row and column labels makes data selection, aggregation, and visualization easier and adds clarity. Beginners may easily incorporate data from many formats into Python by learning how to create DataFrames from several data sources, which lays the groundwork for more complex machine learning projects.

Accessing and modifying data is simple once a DataFrame is established, but it necessitates knowledge of important syntax and techniques. Using their names, DataFrames enable the selection of particular columns, yielding a Series, a pandas object that resembles a one-dimensional array. Rows can be accessed using either label-based indexing with the loc method or integer-based indexing with the iloc method, and a list of column names can be used to choose multiple columns. Additionally, users can filter rows that satisfy specified criteria using Boolean indexing, which is especially helpful for activities like eliminating outliers or choosing data subsets for model training. Because effectively obtaining and manipulating data is a crucial step in preparing datasets for AI algorithms, beginners must become familiar with various indexing strategies to ensure that the correct information is fed into models.

Numerous built-in functions and methods offered by Pandas make typical data operations within DataFrames easier. Data summarization techniques like describe, info, and value counts assist novices in rapidly comprehending the distribution, structure, and quality of their data. Accurate model training depends on users maintaining clean datasets, which is made possible by functions for handling missing values like fillna and dropna. Advanced data manipulations required in machine learning pipelines are made possible by sorting and rating data using sort values and rank, as well as combining or merging several DataFrames using merge or concat. In order to become proficient at cleaning, transforming, and exploring enormous datasets—often the most time-consuming yet crucial aspect of AI and machine learning projects—beginners must practice these procedures.

In order to extract insights from data, DataFrames also offer group-based transformations, arithmetic operations, and aggregation. DataFrames can be directly used for column-wise or row-wise operations, enabling computations such as addition, subtraction, multiplication, and the use of the apply method to apply custom functions. When using the groupby method to group data by one or more columns, statistics like mean, sum, or count may be aggregated for each group, which is very useful when examining patterns or trends in datasets. These processes aid in feature preparation, dataset summarization, and insight generation that guide model creation in AI and machine learning. Early mastery of these methods is beneficial for novices because it lays the groundwork for more complex feature engineering, which is essential to creating successful machine learning models.

Additionally, DataFrames work very well with other libraries and technologies that are frequently used in machine learning and artificial intelligence. Pandas, for example, easily interfaces with Matplotlib or Seaborn for data visualization and with NumPy for effective numerical computations. Before feeding data into scikit-learn, TensorFlow, or PyTorch models, it is frequently necessary to prepare the data in a pandas DataFrame. Models can process structured data effectively by converting DataFrames to NumPy arrays or tensors. The learning curve for AI applications is made more manageable for novices who become proficient in DataFrame manipulation, which allows them to handle datasets of various complexities, from small experimental datasets to large-scale real-world data. Having seamless transitions between pandas and other libraries guarantees that novices can solve issues of any kind or size.

The ability of pandas DataFrames to handle different data types in a single table is another important feature. DataFrames can simultaneously contain numbers, texts, and categorical variables in distinct columns, unlike NumPy arrays, which usually require homogeneous data types. When working with real-world datasets, which frequently contain a variety of data kinds, this flexibility is especially helpful. In order to properly handle these types, beginners need to know how to encode categorical variables, convert columns to the proper data types, and carry out type-specific actions. The dependability of machine learning results is increased, and errors are decreased when data types are handled correctly, which guarantees that models can process and understand the data appropriately.

DataFrames offer ways to quickly summarize and evaluate data, which improves visualization and exploratory data analysis. Plotting functions can be used to generate histograms, scatter plots, or line charts straight from DataFrames, while operations like head and tail let novices preview datasets. Because it enables the discovery of patterns, trends, and anomalies that guide feature engineering and model selection, visual examination of data is crucial to AI and machine learning. In order to comprehend algorithm performance and make wise preprocessing decisions, beginners who use DataFrame-based visualization have an intuitive grasp of how data behaves.

Lastly, learning pandas DataFrames gives novices the ability to write code for AI projects that is efficient, readable, and well-organized. DataFrames reduce complexity and potential errors by offering a consistent framework for data manipulation and storage. Learners can prepare datasets, carry out preprocessing procedures, and incorporate data into machine learning pipelines with confidence if they grasp the fundamentals of building, indexing, modifying, and summarizing DataFrames. Because the concepts of tabular data manipulation, cleaning, and analysis are universal, the knowledge acquired with pandas DataFrames transcends Python and offers a strong basis for dealing with data in any AI or data science setting. By concentrating on the fundamentals of DataFrame, novices gain the necessary skills to progress from basic experimentation to developing comprehensive AI and machine learning solutions.

Data Cleaning Methods

The quality and dependability of the models created are frequently determined by data cleansing, which is an essential phase in the artificial intelligence and machine learning workflow. Inconsistencies, errors, missing values, duplication, and irrelevant information are common in raw datasets, which can have a detrimental impact on model performance. Understanding data cleaning techniques is crucial for Python novices as it serves as the basis for precise analysis, efficient model training, and insightful discoveries. To ensure that the information is consistent, comprehensive, and appropriate for processing by machine learning algorithms, data cleaning entails a number of methodical approaches designed to find and fix these problems. Data that has been properly cleaned lowers noise, increases model accuracy, and expedites deployment and experimentation.

Missing values are among the most prevalent problems in datasets. Numerous factors, such as faults made during data collecting, technology issues, or human input problems, might result in missing data. Since many machine learning algorithms are unable to handle missing values natively, it is imperative that they be addressed. Beginners can deal with missing data in a number of ways. Deletion is one strategy in which any rows or columns with missing values are completely eliminated. Even though this is straightforward, if several entries are missing, a substantial amount of information may be lost. Imputation, which substitutes data for missing values depending on a variety of criteria, is another popular tactic. For example, the mean, median, or mode of the column can be used to substitute numerical values, and the most common category can be used to substitute categorical data. Predictive modeling, which estimates missing values based on associations with other features, is a component of advanced imputation approaches. By comprehending these methods and knowing when to use them, novices may preserve data integrity without needlessly sacrificing dataset size.

Another common problem that needs careful attention is duplicates. Repeated data entry, combining several datasets, or mistakes in data aggregation can result in duplicate records. Duplicates have the potential to distort analysis, inflate statistical metrics, and bias machine learning models if they are not corrected. Python offers techniques for efficiently identifying and eliminating duplicates. In order to eliminate duplicates while preserving the first occurrence or a representative record, novices might utilize routines that detect exact duplicates based on all columns or particular key fields. More sophisticated string matching or similarity metrics are needed to identify near-duplicates, if there are subtle variances or typographical errors. The dataset is cleaned up, and the resulting models are more accurate and dependable when duplicates are removed.

Another issue that frequently arises in real-world datasets is inconsistent data. Differences in naming standards, formats, units, or categorical values are examples of inconsistencies. A dataset might, for instance, have several representations for the same category, such as "USA," "United States," and "US." Standardization, which transforms values into a consistent format, is frequently used to address inconsistencies. Beginners can enforce uniform naming rules, normalize text, and convert units to a common measurement by using string manipulation techniques. By ensuring that algorithms accurately interpret the data, standardization lowers errors and enhances the caliber of analysis. Since machine learning algorithms frequently regard each distinct category as a separate value, and inconsistent representations might produce unexpected categories that mislead models, consistency is especially crucial when it comes to categorical data.

Another feature of data that might skew analysis and model performance is outliers. Extreme values that differ greatly from the rest of the data are known as outliers, and they are frequently the consequence of measurement errors, data entry errors, or inherent variability. Since outliers can have a disproportionate impact on statistical metrics and model training, identifying them is an essential component of data cleaning. To identify outliers, novices can employ statistical approaches like Z-scores, interquartile ranges, or visualization techniques like box plots and scatter plots. Outliers can be eliminated, transformed, or capped once they have been found. When outliers indicate errors, it is appropriate to remove them completely; nevertheless, adjustments like normalization or logarithmic scale can lessen their impact without erasing data. Models are trained on representative data and are resilient to changes in real-world inputs when outliers are handled carefully.

Another crucial component of Python dataset cleaning is data type correction. Columns having inaccurate or inconsistent data types, such as dates displayed as strings or numerical values saved as text, are frequently seen in raw datasets. Accurate calculations, aggregations, and comparisons depend on proper data typing. Python enables novices to methodically examine and transform data types, guaranteeing that date-time columns can be utilized for temporal research and numeric columns are appropriate for mathematical procedures. Errors during preprocessing and modeling can be avoided by converting and validating data types, which facilitates seamless integration with machine learning algorithms that depend on particular data formats.

When preparing datasets, managing noise and irrelevant data is equally crucial. While irrelevant data consists of features or columns that don't offer useful information for the work at hand, noise is defined as random or meaningless oscillations that don't add to a model's prediction ability. Identifiers, metadata, and redundant information are examples of irrelevant features, but sensor failures, human entry errors, or sample variability can all produce noise. To cut down on noise and eliminate unnecessary characteristics, novices can use feature selection, filtering, or smoothing techniques. Models become easier to understand, training becomes more effective, and the chance of overfitting is decreased by concentrating on pertinent, high-quality data.

Managing categorical data and making sure it is appropriately encoded for machine learning models is a crucial component of data cleansing. Since many algorithms need numerical input, encoding techniques are needed to change categorical variables. Label encoding gives each category a numerical value, but one-hot encoding turns each category into a separate binary column, in addition to allowing novices to preserve consistency between training and testing datasets. Proper encoding guarantees that models understand categorical data accurately. Python packages like scikit-learn and pandas offer functions to automate encoding, which makes it simpler for novices to preprocess data without committing mistakes by hand.

Iterative validation and inspection are frequently a part of data cleaning. Novices should take a methodical approach that involves examining the dataset, spotting possible problems, using cleaning methods, and confirming findings. Finding anomalies, missing values, and trends that need attention is made easier with the use of summary functions, descriptive statistics, and visualization tools. Unintended repercussions are less likely when cleaning methods are tested on small groups of data before being applied to the full dataset. Beginners may make sure the dataset is accurate, consistent, and prepared for the creation of machine learning models by closely analyzing and improving the data cleaning procedure.

To sum up, data cleaning is an essential step for Python newbies learning machine learning and artificial intelligence. Learners can create datasets that are dependable, consistent, and appropriate for algorithmic processing by removing noise, irrelevant features, duplicates, inconsistencies, outliers, and erroneous data types. Models are trained on high-quality data when data cleaning techniques are understood and used, which enhances accuracy, robustness, and interpretability. Gaining proficiency in these methods enables novices to manage real-world information efficiently, bridging the gap between unprocessed data and insightful analysis and laying the groundwork for future AI and machine learning initiatives. In addition to expediting the modeling process, efficient data cleaning boosts confidence in the outcomes, freeing up students to concentrate on analyzing algorithms, drawing conclusions, and creating precise and workable solutions.

Exploratory Data Analysis

A crucial phase in the data science and machine learning process, exploratory data analysis, or EDA for short, enables novices to comprehend the structure, quality, and trends in a dataset prior to using any prediction models. The goal of EDA is to obtain insights that direct additional research and model construction, not to draw definitive conclusions. Through meticulous data analysis, students can spot irregularities, missing values, outliers, or discrepancies that might compromise the effectiveness of AI systems. Python offers a robust ecosystem of EDA-facilitating tools, like pandas, NumPy, matplotlib, and seaborn, which make it possible for novices to work with data effectively and see patterns in an understandable way. EDA is a crucial first step for anyone starting their path into AI and machine learning since it helps build a solid foundation for feature engineering, model selection, and algorithm tweaking.

Knowing the dataset's fundamental structure is the initial step in exploratory data analysis. Examining the number of rows and columns, the data types of each feature, and summary statistics like mean, median, minimum, maximum, and standard deviation are common first steps for beginners. This procedure is simple because of Python's pandas library's info, describe, head, and tail methods. Because machine learning algorithms handle numerical and categorical data differently, it is particularly crucial to understand data kinds. Students can rapidly identify features that could need normalization, scaling, or modification with the aid of summary statistics, which offer a high-level perspective of the distribution of data values. Beginners can also confirm that the dataset has been imported correctly by looking at the first rows of data. This gives them a preview of any potential problems, like conflicting naming conventions or formatting difficulties that could make analysis more difficult.

Finding and managing missing data is a crucial part of EDA. Errors in data collection or aggregation frequently result in incomplete entries in datasets, and missing values can have a substantial effect on machine learning models' accuracy. Python offers a number of ways to detect missing data, including isnull and notnull, and visualization tools like bar charts and heatmaps can draw attention to any patterns that are missing from the dataset. In order to deal with missing values, novices must choose methods. These methods could include deleting rows or columns that include a lot of missing data, imputing missing values using the mean, median, or mode, or estimating missing entries using predictive models. In order to guarantee that models are trained on clean and representative datasets, minimize bias, and enhance generalization to new data, it is imperative that missing data be handled properly.

Another crucial component of exploratory data analysis is outlier detection. If left unchecked, outliers—data points that differ substantially from the majority of observations—can skew model predictions. Beginners can find anomalous values or clusters of anomalies with the aid of visual aids such as box plots, scatter plots, and histograms. Statistical techniques, such as the interquartile range or z-scores, offer quantitative tools for identifying outliers. The context of the problem determines how outliers should be handled in AI and machine learning; in some situations, they are errors that need to be eliminated, while in others, they might be uncommon but significant occurrences. Outlier analysis lowers the possibility that models will be fooled by atypical values and guarantees that the dataset represents significant patterns during EDA.

In exploratory data analysis, visualization is essential because it helps novices understand data and find correlations between variables. The distribution of single variables is shown via histograms and density plots, which aid students in comprehending skewness, kurtosis, or other transformations needed for modeling. Feature selection and engineering are guided by the interactions and dependencies between many variables that are revealed via scatter plots, pair plots, and correlation heatmaps. Bar charts and count plots are useful tools for categorical data because they display frequency distributions and offer valuable information on class balance, which is crucial for classification tasks. The matplotlib and seaborn libraries in Python offer versatile and potent tools for producing these visualizations, which facilitate pattern recognition and findings communication for novices. In addition to facilitating well-informed decision-making, visual exploration improves comprehension of the dataset's underlying structure, which is crucial for developing AI and machine learning solutions.

Because they help determine which variables are predictive and which may be redundant, feature connections and correlations are very crucial during EDA. At the same time, pivot tables and cross-tabulations provide light on the interactions between category features, and correlation matrices aid in determining linear relationships between numerical variables. Selecting independent variables for modeling is guided by an understanding of feature interactions, which also points to the need for dimensionality reduction methods like principal component analysis to make large datasets easier to understand. Novices discover that strongly correlated features might cause multicollinearity problems in some methods, which can impact the performance of the model. Learners get a better grasp of which variables contain important information and how they affect the predictive ability of machine learning models by examining feature interactions during exploratory data analysis.

Exploratory data analysis results are frequently used to guide data transformation. For features to be appropriate for machine learning algorithms, they may need to be scaled, normalized, or encoded. Standardization, min-max scaling, and logarithmic transformations can handle skewed distributions or disparate magnitudes, guaranteeing that algorithms understand the data correctly. Encoding techniques like one-hot or label encoding may be necessary for categorical variables in order to translate textual data into numerical representations. EDA makes it possible for novices to determine whether these transformations are necessary, guaranteeing that the dataset is prepared to optimize model performance. Data that has been properly transformed minimizes bias caused by unprocessed characteristics and enhances convergence for algorithms such as gradient descent.

In supervised learning situations, exploratory data analysis also aids novices in determining class balance. Biased models that perform poorly on minority classes might result from imbalanced datasets, in which certain categories have a disproportionately higher number of samples than others. Class imbalances can be detected with the aid of statistical summaries and visualization, and these problems can be resolved by applying remedial strategies, including oversampling, under sampling, or the creation of synthetic data. Learners can create more efficient preprocessing pipelines and choose assessment measures that appropriately represent model performance across all classes by spotting any issues early in the analysis process.

Lastly, for novices in AI and machine learning, exploratory data analysis cultivates an attitude of curiosity, critical thinking, and problem-solving. It invites students to inquire about the dataset, including why particular patterns appear, potential links, and ways to address problems with data quality. EDA gives novices practical experience with Python libraries, helps them develop an intuitive understanding of data behavior, and equips them with abilities that are critical to the machine learning process as a whole. Learners lower the chance of mistakes and improve overall results by carefully examining and comprehending the data prior to modeling. This lays the groundwork for developing more precise, dependable, and interpretable AI solutions.

From Raw Data to Reliable Intelligence

This chapter's real worth is found in the transformation it makes possible, not in the workings of arrays, tables, or charts. Artificial intelligence's ability to make accurate decisions or serve as a deceptive source of confusion depends on how data is handled and prepared. Applying the concepts in this chapter transforms unstructured data into an organized understanding. Decisions are made based on clarity rather than conjecture, patterns become apparent, and discrepancies are addressed. But even the most sophisticated algorithms fall short when ignored. Unreliable results are produced by models that are trained on dirty or misinterpreted data, which magnify mistakes and reinforce prejudice. Poor data preparation can result in financial loss, incorrect diagnoses, ineffective operations, or misdirected tactics in real-world settings like marketing, finance, healthcare, or logistics. The discipline used before the algorithm ever runs is often what makes the difference between success and failure in AI, not the algorithm itself.

Putting these ideas into practice alters your perspective on information. You take your time and examine the accuracy of your inputs rather than jumping right into modeling. You start to examine distributions, check assumptions, investigate missing values, and match data types with their intended uses. This change boosts self-esteem. Predictive accuracy rises, training stability is enhanced, and unexpected model behavior is decreased with clean data. Credibility is also increased. Transparent and repeatable findings are trusted by teams. When projects yield consistent and comprehensible results, stakeholders support them. Data preparation is strategic groundwork, not a preparatory task.

If ignored, the effects build up gradually. Significant distortions are created when minor discrepancies are combined. Results are inflated by duplicate entries. Averages are skewed by outliers. Silent computation errors are caused by incorrect data types. Confusion caused by inconsistent labeling permeates dashboards and reports. Decisions based on faulty analysis eventually result in costly setbacks that cannot be undone. Unreliable data management loses time and damages confidence in a competitive setting. Troubleshooting takes up more team energy than innovation. In addition to the technical cost, there is a reputational penalty.

Think about a real-world example. Consider how a retail business prepares sales information for demand projections. Inconsistent product codes, mixed currency formats, and missing transaction dates are all included in the dataset. Because duplicate records were never eliminated, the forecasting model forecasts inflated demand for some items in the absence of cleaning and exploration. The forecasts closely match actual purchasing trends if organized data preparation is put into practice, including standardizing formats, eliminating duplicates, correctly filling in missing timestamps, and confirming numerical consistency. Within a quarter, inventory waste decreases by 15%. A new model architecture was not the difference. The preparation was methodical.

This is further demonstrated in a short narrative. A patient risk prediction system was once developed by a tiny healthcare startup. The researchers neglected inconsistent data submission among clinics in favor of a heavy focus on model complexity. Some used simplified categorical labels to record blood pressure, while others used millimeters of mercury. Unpredictable risk scores were generated by the program. A data analyst examined the preprocessing step and found the discrepancy after months of perplexity. The model's performance stabilized, and trust was restored after it was standardized and sanitized. The lesson was straightforward but profound: clarity is the foundation of intellect.

Data preparation can be helpfully compared to laying a building's foundation. Cracks and instability are guaranteed by a weak foundation, regardless of how exquisite the building above is. When done correctly, strong foundations are invisible, but they are essential to everything. Robust analysis is supported by clean data, just as tall buildings are supported by reinforced concrete.

You can utilize a straightforward structure known as the CLEAR Process—Collect, Label, Examine, Adjust, and Review—to put what you've learned into practice right away. First, make sure the sources of the data are trustworthy and pertinent by doing responsible data collection. In order to align formats, categories, and units, the second step is to label and structure the data uniformly. Third, use exploratory analysis to look for missing values, abnormalities, and trends in the dataset. Fourth, make adjustments using cleaning methods such as dealing with null values, fixing discrepancies, and getting rid of duplicates. Before beginning modeling, check the dataset once the modifications have been made to ensure its integrity. This methodical procedure creates discipline and avoids hurried analysis.

By the end of this chapter, you will know how to use arrays and dataframes to convert unstructured datasets into formats that are ready for analysis. You will be able to recognize and address typical problems with data quality that jeopardize model reliability at the end of this chapter. You will be able to use exploratory analysis to find significant trends and identify anomalies by the end of this chapter. You will be able to create a repeatable preparatory process that boosts AI project productivity and consistency by the end of this chapter. Instead of assuming a dataset is prepared for modeling, you will be able to determine whether it is by the end of this chapter.

Disciplined data handling has practical applications beyond AI initiatives. It fosters critical thinking. It makes one more meticulous. It increases resistance to false information. The capacity to challenge, purify, and make sense of information becomes a competitive advantage at a time when data streams are abundant. Because their ideas are based on solid evidence, organizations that are adept at preparation make decisions more quickly and intelligently.

Think carefully about how you handle data and information before proceeding. Consider this: Where in my existing workflow do I make hasty preparations rather than giving them thorough thought? Which persistent data problems have I normalized rather than fixed? How may my previous projects' accuracy change with better data discipline? Which mechanisms can I put in place right now to validate and standardize incoming data? If I shared a standardized framework for data preparation with my organization, who would gain the most?

Complex neural networks and sophisticated optimization methods are not the first steps toward mastering artificial intelligence. Respect for data is the first step. Your models react reliably when you handle data with care. If you ignore it, your systems will reflect that disregard. Every subsequent project's results are shaped by the habits developed during preparation. This is when the decision between flimsy forecasts and reliable intelligence begins.

CHAPTER III

Mathematical Foundations for AI

Vectors and Matrices

In mathematics, vectors and matrices are basic ideas that are essential to machine learning and artificial intelligence. In order to develop algorithms that process, analyze, and learn from information, they offer a framework for structured data representation and manipulation. Since vectors and matrices are the fundamental building blocks of many machine learning models, such as neural networks, clustering algorithms, and linear regression, it is imperative that beginners in Python understand them. Quantities with both magnitude and direction are represented by vectors, which are essentially ordered lists of numbers. This idea is extended by matrices, which are two-dimensional arrays of integers that permit operations that facilitate model computations and transformations by organizing and manipulating data in rows and columns.

A vector is one-dimensional and can represent various types of data in machine learning. One data point's feature values, for instance, can be stored in a vector, where each element represents a distinct measurement or attribute. In machine learning models, vectors are also used to represent weights; each vector element represents a parameter that influences the model's predictions. Arrays from the NumPy module are an effective way to represent vectors in Python, enabling quick computation and manipulation. The fast implementation of linear transformations, similarity metrics, and optimization algorithms is made possible by the element-wise or mathematically defined execution of operations on vectors, including addition, subtraction, scalar multiplication, and dot products. Since these operations are fundamental to knowing how models handle information, beginners should concentrate on comprehending how they impact the data.

Matrices are useful for describing datasets, transformations, and relationships between variables because they allow vectors to be extended into two dimensions. In a matrix, each column denotes a feature or trait, and each row typically represents a single data point. Matrix storage, weight matrices for linear models, and transformation matrices for data pretreatment and dimensionality reduction are all utilized in machine learning. AI algorithms rely heavily on linear algebra calculations, which are made easier by matrices. NumPy arrays are an effective way to perform matrix addition, subtraction, and multiplication in Python. These operations adhere to certain principles. Beginners can manipulate big datasets, carry out feature engineering, and design models that depend on linear feature combinations by having a basic understanding of matrix operations.

The dot product, which calculates the similarity between two vectors and serves as the foundation for many machine learning calculations, is one of the most significant operations combining vectors and matrices. The dot product creates a scalar value that represents the magnitude and direction relationship between two vectors by multiplying their respective elements and adding the results. This process is essential to neural networks, which use it to compute activations at each layer, and linear regression, which uses it to compute predictions. The corresponding operation for matrices is matrix multiplication, which enables the meaningful combination of parameters and data. In order to create a new matrix that represents coupled transformations, matrix multiplication requires that the number of columns in the first matrix and the number of rows in the second matrix coincide. In order to properly develop algorithms, beginners need to be aware of the dimensional limits and implications of matrix multiplication.

Another crucial function in matrix manipulation is transposition. When a matrix is transposed, rows become columns and vice versa by flipping it over its diagonal. This operation is frequently used in machine learning to reorganize data during preprocessing or align matrices in operations like matrix multiplication. For instance, weight matrices may need to be transposed in some neural network operations in order to conform to the input vectors' shape. NumPy makes transposition in Python easy, and once mastered, it enables novices to execute more intricate data transformations accurately and rapidly. Systems of linear equations, which are commonly seen in regression models and optimization issues, can also be solved using transpose procedures.

Vectors and matrices offer a variety of mathematical functions that are crucial for AI and machine learning, in addition to basic operations. For example, norms quantify distances, normalize data, or regularize models to avoid overfitting. They do this by measuring the size of vectors. Determinants and inverses are crucial in matrix analysis for understanding features like matrix rank and singularity, solving linear equations, and computing transformations. In dimensionality reduction methods such as principal component analysis, eigenvalues and eigenvectors offer essential information about the inherent structure of matrices. Since many algorithms implicitly rely on these mathematical features during computation, it is easier for novices to use machine learning libraries when they understand these notions in the context of Python.

In machine learning applications like image processing, natural language processing, and sensor data analysis, vectors and matrices are also essential for expressing higher-dimensional data. Multiple images can be represented as a three-dimensional array or tensor, and images, for instance, can be represented as matrices where each element corresponds to a pixel value. Numerical vectors that represent word counts, frequencies, or embeddings can be created from text data and processed as matrices for model input. Beginners may efficiently handle complicated datasets by learning how to organize and manipulate these structures in Python, converting raw data into formats appropriate for model training and evaluation.

With built-in functions for array generation, arithmetic, and linear algebra operations, and applying transformations across datasets, Python libraries such as NumPy make it easier to create and work with vectors and matrices. These tools enable novices to efficiently construct vector and matrix operations without the need for manual computation or explicit loops. Additionally, NumPy offers broadcasting, which improves code clarity and performance by enabling operations on vectors and matrices of various shapes without the need for explicit reshaping. Beginners can concentrate on the reasoning behind algorithms and the interpretation of outcomes instead of the finer points of implementation by utilizing these skills.

The efficient use of vectors and matrices in machine learning workflows is intimately related to feature engineering, model implementation, and data preprocessing. Structured vector and matrix operations are essential for combining datasets, making predictions, normalizing characteristics, and calculating distances. Beginners can create effective data pipelines, test out various model architectures, and accurately assess performance by knowing how to work with these structures. Additionally, mastering these ideas lays a solid basis for more complex subjects like tensor operations in deep learning frameworks, where multi-dimensional arrays apply the concepts of matrices and vectors to higher-order data.

To sum up, the foundation of numerical representation and computation in AI and machine learning is made up of vectors and matrices. While matrices structure datasets, transformations, and relationships between variables, vectors enable novices to represent individual data points, features, and parameters. Implementing algorithms and carrying out efficient data analysis requires a solid understanding of operations such as addition, subtraction, dot products, multiplication, transposition, and norms. Beginners may concentrate on comprehending the fundamentals of machine learning instead of being bogged down by intricate calculations, thanks to Python's NumPy library, which offers effective and user-friendly tools for creating, manipulating, and analyzing vectors and matrices. Gaining expertise with vectors and matrices helps students bridge the gap between mathematical theory and real-world application by giving them the fundamental abilities needed to handle data, train models, and investigate the many applications in artificial intelligence. Beginners may confidently tackle more complex subjects and use Python's capabilities in practical machine learning applications by developing a solid grasp of these ideas early on.

Probability Theory Basics

A key idea in AI and machine learning, probability theory serves as the foundation for comprehending uncertainty, forecasting outcomes, and simulating intricate systems. Learning the fundamentals of probability gives novices a strong basis for analyzing data, creating algorithms, and putting machine learning models into practice that can make wise choices in unpredictable situations. Fundamentally, probability quantifies the possibility that occurrences will transpire within a specified sample space.

Whereas the sample space includes every conceivable result of a random experiment, an event reflects a particular outcome or combination of results. Beginners may measure uncertainty and cultivate an intuition for probabilistic thinking by comprehending these fundamental ideas. This is crucial for AI applications like categorization, prediction, and decision-making under uncertainty.

A number between zero and one, where zero denotes impossibility and one denotes certainty, is commonly used to express the likelihood of an event. Counting the favorable outcomes and dividing by the entire number of outcomes in the sample space is a common method for calculating the probability of simple events. On a typical six-sided dice, for instance, the odds of rolling a certain number are one out of six, or roughly 0.167. Beginners must realize that probability is a reflection of the likelihood based on the experiment's conditions and assumptions rather than a static metric. This idea readily applies to more complicated AI scenarios, such as forecasting the possibility of a disease developing, the probability of a particular image containing a specific object, or the probability of customer attrition. Machine learning models may make judgments based on the inherent uncertainty of real-world data when they have a thorough understanding of probability in these situations.

The differentiation between independent and dependent events is a fundamental concept in probability theory. Independent events are ones whose occurrence has no bearing on the likelihood that another event will occur. For instance, flipping a coin twice results in independent events since the first flip's result has no bearing on the second. Dependent events, on the other hand, occur when the occurrence of one event influences the probability of another. Because it provides the foundation for modeling the interactions between variables in AI and machine learning, beginners need to be aware of this distinction. A key component of modeling dependent events is conditional probability, which measures the likelihood of an event provided that another event has already occurred. For instance, the sensitivity and specificity of the test determine the likelihood that a patient has a condition in the context of medical diagnosis if the test is positive. Implementing algorithms like Naive Bayes classifiers, which mostly rely on probabilistic correlations between features and outcomes, requires an understanding of conditional probability.

The foundation for determining the probabilities of combined events is provided by the laws of probability, which include the addition and multiplication rules. The multiplication rule determines the likelihood that both occurrences will occur at the same time, whereas the addition rule determines the likelihood that either of the two events will occur. These principles form the basis for both building probability distributions that explain the behavior of random variables and reasoning about many events. Because it offers a straightforward way to compute probabilities indirectly, beginners should also familiarize themselves with complementary probability, which quantifies the possibility that an event does not occur. When students understand these guidelines, they may approach difficult probabilistic challenges methodically, which guarantees accurate data interpretation and well-informed AI application decision-making.

Another fundamental idea in probability theory is random variables, which are numerical representations of random events. Random variables can be continuous, meaning they can take on an unlimited number of values within a range, or discrete, meaning they can take on a finite or countable set of values. At the same time, continuous random variables model metrics like height, temperature, or stock prices; discrete random variables are frequently used to model counts or categorical outcomes, such as the number of defective products in a batch. Understanding and simulating uncertainty requires the use of probability distributions, which outline the likelihood of each potential value of a random variable. The uniform, binomial, and normal distributions are among the most frequent distributions that beginners come across; each has special qualities that make it appropriate for various AI and machine learning applications. For instance, many machine learning assumptions and methods are based on the normal distribution, which is also frequently used in statistical modeling.

The statistical metrics of expectation, variance, and standard deviation are obtained from probability distributions that depict how random variables behave. Variance quantifies the spread or dispersion of the values around the mean, whereas the expected value, or mean, gives the average result over a large number of trials. The square root of variance, or standard deviation, provides a comprehensible indicator of variability. These ideas are essential for novices to comprehend the behavior of data and the quantification of uncertainty. Expectation and variance are important concepts in machine learning that are used to analyze model performance, comprehend prediction intervals, and gauge the dependability of probabilistic models. Beginners may effectively assess data distributions and make well-informed modeling decisions by learning how to compute and interpret these measures.

A fundamental component of probability theory, the Bayes theorem has numerous uses in artificial intelligence and machine learning. It offers a way to update probabilities in light of fresh data, which serves as the foundation for Bayesian inference. The Bayes theorem uses the likelihood of the data given the hypothesis and the prior probability of the hypothesis to quantify the probability of a hypothesis given observed data. This paradigm enables AI models to manage uncertainty, take into account past knowledge, and modify predictions in response to new information. Naive Bayes classifiers, which use Bayes' theorem under the presumption of feature independence to efficiently classify data, are frequently encountered by novices studying probability. Gaining knowledge of the Bayes theorem gives students strong tools for making decisions, seeing patterns, and using probabilistic modeling in a variety of AI applications, such as spam detection and medical diagnostics.

More complex ideas like joint, marginal, and conditional distributions—all crucial for multivariate data analysis—are also supported by probability theory. Marginal distributions give the probability of a single variable without taking other variables into account, whereas joint distributions represent the chance of two or more random variables happening together. The probability of one variable given the values of other variables is the main focus of conditional distributions. These ideas enable novices to build probabilistic graphical models such as Bayesian networks, which express interactions between several variables in an organized way, comprehend correlations, and model complex dependencies. Gaining an understanding of joint, marginal, and conditional distributions is essential to creating AI systems that can effectively handle linked data and reason under uncertainty.

Along with theoretical comprehension, beginners' learning is reinforced by real-world applications of probability in Python. Functions for simulating random occurrences, computing probabilities, creating random variables, and computing statistical measures are available in Python libraries like NumPy, SciPy, and pandas. Programmatically simulating experiments, like rolling dice or flipping coins, aids novices in understanding the law of large numbers, which asserts that the average of numerous independent trials converges to the predicted value, and in developing intuition for probability concepts. Through these hands-on activities, students may effectively use probabilistic models and analyze real-world data, bridging the gap between theory and practice.

In conclusion, the fundamentals of probability theory offer the necessary framework for comprehending uncertainty, formulating forecasts, and putting machine learning algorithms into practice. Sample spaces, events, conditional probability, random variables, probability distributions, expectation, variance, and the Bayes theorem are some of the concepts that give novices the skills they need to do thorough data analysis and interpretation. By grasping these concepts, students may build probabilistic models, assess forecasts, and create AI systems that function dependably in unpredictable situations. Beginners can develop the abilities needed to handle challenging data-driven situations and set the stage for more in-depth research in artificial intelligence and machine learning by fusing theoretical knowledge with real-world Python applications.

Statistical Measures

In artificial intelligence and machine learning, statistical metrics are essential tools for comprehending and evaluating data. Understanding these ideas is crucial for Python novices as they lay the groundwork for deciphering datasets, spotting trends, and getting data ready for modeling. Learners can use statistical measures to compare groups, identify anomalies, summarize and characterize data concisely, and make well-informed judgments regarding data transformation or preprocessing. Before using machine learning algorithms, it is crucial to evaluate the quality of the data and draw relevant conclusions, both of which are challenging without a solid understanding of statistical metrics.

The mean, sometimes referred to as the average, is a fundamental statistical metric that establishes a center value around which data points are dispersed. Using functions from libraries like NumPy or Pandas, computing the mean in Python is simple. Understanding the typical behavior or trend in the data is made easier with the help of the mean, which provides an overview of the dataset. The mean is frequently used in conjunction with other metrics, though, because it can be sensitive to outliers or extreme values. A few very high earnings, for instance, could distort the mean when examining the income of a group of people, giving the impression that it is larger than what is normal for the majority of the group. Although the mean is instructive, novices should be aware that in order to comprehend the data fully, it must be evaluated in relation to other metrics.

Another important statistical metric that shows the center value in an ordered dataset is the median. The median is a trustworthy measure of central tendency in datasets with extreme values because, in contrast to the mean, it is resistant to outliers and skewed distributions. The median offers a more realistic representation of the worth of a normal property, for instance, when examining housing prices, as a small number of luxury houses may significantly surpass average values. Built-in functions in Python that automatically sort data and locate the center point can be used to calculate the median. Novices should understand that combining the mean and median provides information about the data distribution, indicating if it is symmetrical, skewed, or has abnormalities that need to be addressed.

For categorical or discrete data, the mode—the value that appears most frequently in the dataset—is especially helpful. The mode can show which category or choice is most prevalent in datasets that include survey responses, product preferences, or classifications. Python has routines to determine the mode and can provide a list of the most common items when there are many values with the same frequency. In machine learning, feature selection, encoding techniques, and model building can be informed by an understanding of the mode, which aids novices in spotting trends, well-liked features, or dominant behaviors in the data.

Measures of dispersion shed light on how data varies or spreads around center values. Two popular metrics for assessing dispersion are variance and standard deviation. By calculating the average squared departure from the mean, variance gives an indication of the overall degree of divergence of the data points. The data is easier to read because the standard deviation, which is the square root of variance, expresses variability in the same units as the data. These metrics can be effectively calculated in Python with the help of tools like Pandas and NumPy. Since variance and standard deviation show how closely or loosely data points are packed around the mean, it is crucial for novices to comprehend them. Low variability denotes consistency, which can make analysis and prediction easier, but high variability suggests a large range of values, which may impact the stability of models.

The range, which denotes the difference between a dataset's maximum and minimum values, is another crucial statistical concept. Despite its simplicity, the range gives a fast idea of the data's range. It should, however, be evaluated in conjunction with other measures of dispersion since, like the mean, it can be sensitive to outliers. Python has simple techniques for figuring out the maximum and minimum values, making it possible to quickly evaluate the data's general distribution. For novices, knowing the range aids in seeing possible irregularities and comprehending the dataset's size, both of which are important for feature scaling and normalization in machine learning processes.

Other methods that break the data into intervals for more accurate distribution analysis are quantiles and percentiles. Whereas percentiles divide the data into 100 equal parts, quartiles divide the dataset into four equal parts, indicating the lower, middle, and upper values that divide the data. These metrics aid in determining the concentration of values within particular ranges and comprehending the relative positions of data points. Python packages offer routines for quickly calculating quartiles and percentiles, allowing novices to examine datasets for skewness, outliers, or value grouping. In AI and machine learning projects, these metrics are very helpful for feature engineering, risk assessment, and anomaly identification.

Two metrics that quantify the relationship between two or more variables are correlation and covariance. Covariance shows how much two variables change together, although it is difficult to interpret because its magnitude varies depending on the variables' units. Contrarily, correlation standardizes the link and yields a value between -1 and 1 that represents the association's strength and direction. Negative correlation denotes an adverse link, whereas positive correlation shows that as one measure rises, the other tends to rise as well. Python novices can analyze links between several features by computing correlation matrices, which offer information about dependencies that guide feature selection, dimensionality reduction, and model creation. Preventing multicollinearity in models and selecting variables that offer distinct and significant information requires an understanding of correlation.

Two statistical metrics that characterize a distribution's form are skewness and kurtosis. Kurtosis characterizes how heavy the tails are in relation to a normal distribution, whereas skewness shows whether the data is symmetric or has a lengthy tail in one direction. These metrics aid novices in comprehending departures from normalcy, which might affect algorithm performance and selection. Many machine learning models, for instance, rely on the assumption that input features are normal; skewed data may need to be transformed using techniques like normalization or logarithmic scaling. By calculating skewness and kurtosis using Python packages, students can examine the distributional characteristics of their datasets and implement suitable preprocessing methods.

Another effective method for comprehending data is the visualization of statistical metrics. Beginners can visually observe core tendencies, spread, and correlations between variables with the help of techniques like scatter plots, box plots, and histograms. These visual aids enhance numerical measurements and offer a clear grasp of intricate information. Plotting functions in Python libraries like Matplotlib, Seaborn, and Pandas allow students to create understandable and instructive representations, facilitating exploratory data analysis and directing the feature engineering and data cleaning procedures.

To sum up, statistical measurements are essential for Python novices who want to become proficient in machine learning and artificial intelligence. While correlation and shape analysis uncover linkages and patterns that inform modeling choices, measures of central tendency, dispersion, and distribution offer crucial insights into datasets. Learners can efficiently preprocess data, spot abnormalities, choose significant characteristics, and correctly interpret outcomes by comprehending and utilizing these metrics. Python gives novices the ability to properly study and comprehend datasets by offering effective tools and libraries for computing and visualizing these statistical metrics. Gaining proficiency in statistical measurements provides a solid basis for applying machine learning algorithms successfully, allowing students to convert unprocessed data into useful insights and create accurate, comprehensible, and trustworthy models. In addition to improving technical proficiency, statistical literacy cultivates critical thinking, which is crucial for solving problems and making decisions in AI-driven applications.

Derivatives and Optimization

In artificial intelligence and machine learning, derivatives and optimization are key ideas that serve as the mathematical foundation for many algorithms that let computers learn from data. Understanding these subjects is crucial for novices as they offer the means to modify models, reduce mistakes, and enhance forecasts in a methodical manner. A derivative shows how quickly a function changes in relation to one of its variables, providing information on how slight adjustments to the input impact the result. Derivatives are employed in machine learning to ascertain the extent and direction of model parameter modifications required to attain peak performance. Techniques like gradient descent, the main approach for training models like logistic regression, deep neural networks, and linear regression, rely heavily on the idea of a derivative. Gaining an intuitive knowledge of derivatives helps beginners comprehend how algorithms follow a function's slope to iteratively arrive at the optimum answer.

Calculus is where the basic concept of derivatives originates, as the derivative of a function at a specific moment quantifies its instantaneous rate of change. To put it practically, if a model makes predictions based on specific inputs, the derivative indicates how much the forecast would alter if the input were slightly changed. The rate of change with regard to each variable separately, while holding the others constant, is measured for multivariable functions using partial derivatives. In machine learning, where models frequently have several parameters that must be improved at once, this idea is very crucial. Beginners who understand partial derivatives can better understand how each parameter affects prediction error and how to adjust these parameters to reduce it.

The process of determining the optimal collection of parameters that minimizes or maximizes a specific objective function—often referred to as the loss or cost function—is known as optimization in machine learning. As a gauge of model performance, the loss function measures the discrepancy between expected and actual values. The gradient, or vector pointing in the direction of the loss function's sharpest increase, can be found by applying derivatives. Algorithms in training models usually follow the negative gradient direction because the objective is to minimize the loss function. One of the most popular optimization methods is gradient descent, in which parameters are iteratively updated by shifting them slightly in the direction that minimizes the loss. The size of each step, which is dictated by the learning rate, is crucial for beginners to understand. If the step is too small, the model will converge slowly; if it is too large, it may overshoot the minimum or not converge at all.

Gradient descent comes in a variety of forms to accommodate various learning situations. Although batch gradient descent uses the full dataset to compute the gradient, it can be computationally costly for big datasets, but it guarantees a steady update direction. One data point at a time is used by stochastic gradient descent to update parameters; this method offers faster updates but adds noise to the optimization process. By employing small data batches, mini-batch gradient descent achieves a balance between increasing convergence speed and preserving more consistent updates. Understanding these variations is beneficial for beginners because the effectiveness and precision of machine learning model training are impacted by the optimization strategy chosen. Learners may readily implement these techniques with the help of Python libraries like NumPy and TensorFlow, giving them hands-on experience with derivative-based optimization.

Additionally, derivatives are crucial to sophisticated optimization methods used in machine learning. For instance, the Hessian matrix, which is a representation of second-order derivatives, describes the curvature of a function and gives information on the gradient's rate of change. Second-order derivative calculations are computationally demanding, but they are useful for techniques like Newton's optimization, which in some circumstances can converge more quickly than gradient descent. Understanding these ideas helps beginners better appreciate how various optimization techniques affect model training and identify circumstances in which simple gradient descent might not be enough.

Another idea that is strongly related to optimization and derivatives is regularization. By prohibiting unreasonably high parameter values, regularization approaches like L1 and L2 penalties add terms to the loss function to avoid overfitting. The optimization process is guided by the derivatives of these updated loss functions, which strike a balance between properly fitting the data and preserving the simplicity of the model. In order to comprehend how derivatives and loss functions work together to control model complexity and improve generalization to new data, beginners studying optimization in Python frequently attempt to develop regularized models. This knowledge is essential for creating machine learning models that function well in real-world applications as well as on training data.

Beginners can better understand the relationship between derivatives and optimization with the aid of visualization. Plotting a basic loss function versus model parameters enables students to observe how the function's slope suggests which direction to change the parameters. Minima, maxima, or saddle points are those where the derivative is zero. The objective of optimization is to find minima, which are parameter values that reduce the error. Functions, gradients, and iterative updates can be visualized with Python modules like matplotlib, which reinforce theoretical ideas with real-world examples. Beginners can develop their intuition regarding the operation of derivative-based techniques and how optimization directs model training with the aid of these visuals.

Derivatives and optimization are important in unsupervised learning and reinforcement learning, in addition to supervised learning. To reduce the distances between points and cluster centroids, optimization techniques are employed in clustering algorithms such as k-means. Derivatives are employed in reinforcement learning to compute gradients for policy optimization, which aids agents in learning tactics that optimize cumulative rewards. Derivatives are extensively useful and versatile in AI research since even beginners who comprehend them in the context of optimization may apply the same principles across different machine learning paradigms.

Understanding derivatives is also helpful for troubleshooting and error analysis. Analyzing gradients and the behavior of the loss function might reveal possible problems when a model does not converge or generates subpar predictions. In deep learning, issues like vanishing or bursting gradients occur when derivatives are either too tiny or too large, which results in inefficient parameter updates. Studying these situations gives novices a hands-on understanding of how derivative-based optimization can work or not, equipping them to identify and enhance model training techniques.

In conclusion, optimization and derivatives are essential to machine learning because they offer a methodical way to modify model parameters for better performance. Beginners may implement, troubleshoot, and optimize models in Python by comprehending the concepts of derivatives, gradients, loss functions, and iterative optimization techniques like gradient descent. Understanding regularization, sophisticated optimization variations, and partial and second-order derivatives gives students the skills they need to work with complicated models and big datasets. Beginners can gain an intuitive understanding of how machine learning algorithms learn from data through visualization and real-world applications, which strengthens theoretical principles. For anyone beginning in the field of artificial intelligence and machine learning, mastery of optimization and derivatives is crucial since it provides a solid basis for moving on to more complex subjects.

Understanding Loss Functions

Anyone starting out in the field of artificial intelligence and machine learning must grasp the idea of loss functions. A loss function is a mathematical technique used in machine learning to assess how well a model predicts the actual results. It acts as a guide for enhancing model performance during training and gives an indication of the errors the model is making. Understanding loss functions is crucial for novices since it serves as the basis for model optimization, selection, and assessment. Determining whether a model is learning efficiently or how to modify it to get better predictions is challenging without a thorough understanding of loss functions.

Fundamentally, a loss function computes the discrepancy between actual and expected values. The more closely the model's predictions match the real data, the smaller the loss. On the other hand, a higher loss denotes a higher degree of mistake and identifies the areas in which the model has to be improved. Python's built-in functions for effectively computing loss are utilized in conjunction with machine learning libraries and frameworks like scikit-learn, TensorFlow, and PyTorch. These solutions are useful for beginners since they eliminate the need for manual calculations and enable experimentation and comprehension of how various loss functions impact model training. Instant feedback on a model's performance and if learning process modifications are required can be obtained by using Python to track changes in loss throughout training.

The kind of problem being solved determines which of the several loss function types should be used. Mean squared error and mean absolute error are typical loss functions for regression tasks, which entail predicting continuous variables. The average of the squares of the variations between expected and actual values is determined by mean squared error. When significant variations are especially undesired, it can be helpful to square the differences in order to highlight greater inaccuracies. Conversely, mean absolute error provides a more balanced metric that is less susceptible to severe outliers by averaging the absolute differences. To discover how these loss functions affect model performance and how each highlights certain facets of prediction accuracy, beginners can experiment with them.

Loss functions assume a different form for classification problems when the objective is to forecast discrete categories. When dealing with binary and multiclass classification problems, cross-entropy loss is frequently employed. It calculates the discrepancy between the actual distribution of class labels and the projected probability distribution. A high cross-entropy loss suggests that the model has to be adjusted because the predicted probability deviates greatly from the true labels. Beginners may see how the model modifies its parameters during training to minimize the loss and provide more accurate predictions by using Python's cross-entropy loss. Hinge loss is another classification loss function that penalizes predictions that are inaccurate or fall within a margin of error. It is frequently employed in support vector machines. Beginners can more successfully comprehend model results and select suitable evaluation criteria by having a better understanding of these classification loss functions.

Advanced machine learning applications employ specific loss functions in addition to the conventional regression and classification losses. For example, bespoke loss functions may be created to enforce unique constraints or capture particular data features in tasks like image production or anomaly detection. Learners must comprehend the interplay between different losses because generative adversarial networks employ a combination of loss functions for the discriminator and generator models. Similarly, regularization approaches in neural networks guide the model to better generalize to unseen data by adding new terms to the loss function to avoid overfitting. Python packages offer versatile tools for designing, altering, and computing bespoke losses, making it beneficial for novices investigating these complex ideas to experiment with loss functions.

At the core of model training are optimization procedures, which also depend on loss functions. Algorithms like gradient descent modify model parameters during training in order to minimize the loss function. The direction and size of the adjustments required to lower error are indicated by the gradient of the loss function with respect to the model parameters. Since it connects the idea of loss with model learning, it is crucial for novices to comprehend how loss drives parameter changes. Learners can identify problems like slow learning or divergence, comprehend the model's convergence, and make well-informed decisions on hyperparameter tweaking, learning rates, and model architectural modifications by tracking how the loss drops across training epochs in Python.

Beginners can effectively build intuition regarding model performance by visualizing loss during training. It is possible to determine if the model is learning, overfitting, or underfitting by plotting the loss against training iterations. While a loss curve that fluctuates or plateaus may signal the need for additional tuning or an alternative model design, a loss curve that decreases gradually shows good learning. These visualizations are simple to create with Python tools like Matplotlib and Seaborn, which help students understand complex processes intuitively. Additionally, visual feedback reinforces the significance of selecting and tracking suitable loss measures by assisting novices in making the connection between theoretical knowledge of loss functions and real-world results.

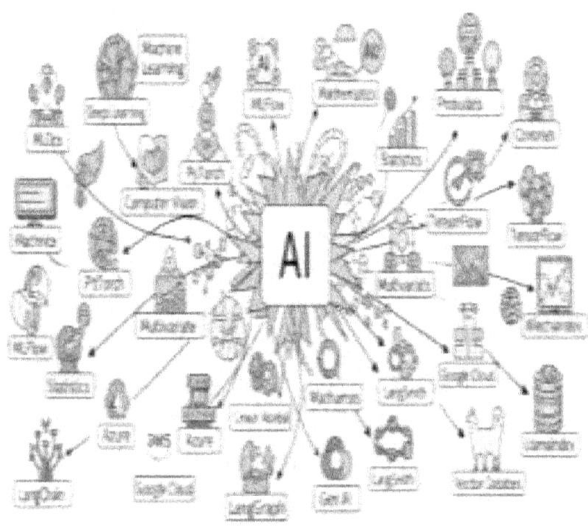

Loss functions can be used in conjunction with metrics to measure prediction error and offer a thorough assessment framework. Evaluation metrics like accuracy, precision, recall, or R-squared offer comprehensible data to gauge model performance, while loss functions direct the optimization process. Beginners should be aware of the difference between metrics and loss functions, as the former provide insight into the efficacy of the model, while the latter make it clear that minimizing loss is a process. Learners can monitor training progress and evaluate practical performance on real-world data by using Python to compute both loss and metrics.

In conclusion, for Python novices who want to advance their knowledge of artificial intelligence and machine learning, a comprehension of loss functions is essential. Loss functions impact algorithm design, direct model optimization, and quantify prediction inaccuracy. They shed light on model performance and learning dynamics, whether they are used for regression, classification, or complex machine learning tasks. Beginners gain a better understanding of how models evolve over time by playing with loss functions, visualizing loss curves, and connecting loss to optimization procedures. Gaining an understanding of loss functions helps students develop their technical skills as well as their analytical thinking, which helps them create, train, and assess models efficiently. Beginners can convert theoretical knowledge into useful abilities that serve as the basis for more complex machine learning and artificial intelligence applications by using Python's tools and frameworks to investigate these ideas practically.

The Architecture of Intelligent Thinking

The framework that enables intelligent systems is mathematics, not just a necessary condition for artificial intelligence. Students are not just collecting formulas when they have completed studying vectors, matrices, probability, statistics, derivatives, optimization, and loss functions. Their ability to confidently and successfully develop, assess, and enhance intelligent systems is determined by the mental architecture they are creating. This chapter is significant because it turns artificial intelligence from a mystery concept into a quantifiable one. These mathematical underpinnings, when used, enable you to analyze model behavior, identify problems, improve performance, and engage in responsible innovation. Ignoring AI reduces it to guesswork; models turn into black boxes, judgments into presumptions, and progress into blind trial-and-error. Misunderstanding the mathematics can result in ineffective systems, skewed forecasts, or expensive errors in real-world settings where AI affects financial approvals, medical diagnostics, logistical planning, and recommendation systems.

Your attitude to problem-solving fundamentally alters when you put these ideas into practice. You start by asking why a model works rather than if it does. You use optimization logic rather than making haphazard changes to the settings. Errors are interpreted quantitatively rather than emotionally. You can quantify risk clearly, forecast consequences before deployment, and systematically improve performance if you are mathematically literate. On the other hand, weak systems result from neglecting their underpinnings. Because probability distributions change in real-world scenarios, a model may seem accurate when tested but fall short. In the absence of statistical metrics, noise could be mistaken for a signal. If you don't understand optimization and derivatives, you might never figure out why a model overfits or converges too slowly. Stronger decision-making, fewer mistakes, quicker iteration cycles, and more reliable AI systems are the immediate and practical effects.

Think about a real-world example. Consider developing a predictive model to estimate a retail company's monthly product demand. Your input data is structured using matrices and vectors. Demand uncertainty can be quantified with the aid of probability theory. Seasonality trends are revealed by statistical measurements like mean and variance. Optimization techniques that modify model parameters are guided by derivatives. The discrepancy between expected demand and actual sales is measured by the loss function. Understanding each element can help you determine whether forecasting errors are caused by imbalanced data, improper learning rates, or ill-defined loss criteria. Without that knowledge, you could make expensive inventory decisions and mistakenly interpret swings as failures.

This is clarified via a little illustrative tale. Marco, a young data analyst, was given the task of enhancing a recommendation system. At first, he approached the model as he would a vending machine: change a parameter, see the result, and repeat. He became frustrated when his performance gradually improved. He once hurried through the mathematical foundations, but one day he went back to them. He started to see gradients as slopes leading him downhill toward ideal solutions, vectors as directions in space, and probabilities as quantifiable confidence. He strategically changed the learning rate and looked at the gradient of the loss function rather than adjusting the parameters at random. The accuracy of the system significantly increased in a few weeks. Marco saw that the map had always been mathematics; he had only not mastered its interpretation.

This understanding can be anchored by a clear metaphor. AI's mathematical underpinnings are comparable to a skyscraper's foundation. The deeper and more robust the basis, the higher you wish to build. Once the building is tall, you might not notice the foundation, but without it, the entire thing gives way under stress. Similar to this, sophisticated AI methods like generative models, deep learning architectures, and reinforcement learning systems rely only on these mathematical foundations. Progress stops or fails in their absence.

You can use a straightforward structure known as the CALM Method—Clarify, Analyze, Learn, and Modify—to turn this information into action. By specifying what your model is optimizing and which loss function denotes success, you can first make the goal more clear. Second, use statistical methods to analyze the data in order to comprehend correlations, variance, and distribution. Third, minimize loss through optimization by using gradient-based techniques and derivatives. Fourth, make systematic rather than haphazard changes to features, learning rates, or model structure in response to quantifiable outcomes. Every improvement step is guaranteed to be based on mathematical reasoning with this approach.

You will be able to convert real-world data into vector and matrix representations that are appropriate for machine learning models at the end of this chapter. You will be able to assess the dependability and degree of uncertainty in AI predictions by the end of this chapter by interpreting probability and statistical measurements. You will be able to describe how optimization methods and derivatives enhance model performance by the end of this chapter. You will be able to choose and evaluate suitable loss functions to match AI systems with intended results at the end of this chapter. You will be able to identify performance problems with mathematical reasoning instead of conjecture by the end of this chapter.

Using this chapter has practical applications outside of technical projects. It affects your trustworthiness in the workplace. Teams have faith in experts who can provide proof to support their conclusions. Practitioners who can clearly communicate risk and performance are valued by organizations. Customers depend on predictable, clear models. Because mathematical fluency enables you to explain not just what your model does, but also why it does it, it improves communication.

There are repercussions for disregarding this basis. Uncertainty becomes invisible in the absence of probability. Patterns remain buried in the absence of statistical measures. Optimization is ineffective without derivatives. Performance is aimless without lost functions. These discrepancies undermine credibility in addition to technical accuracy. Projects take longer. Errors keep happening. Trust is undermined. Understanding mathematics is essential—it is protective—in a world where artificial intelligence is influencing society more and more.

Choose one AI project you are planning or working on right now to get started. Determine the loss function and note its precise measurements. To comprehend the distribution of your dataset, compute a minimum of two statistical metrics. During training, visualize the movement of parameter updates along the gradient. Consider whether your optimization procedure is random or systematic. You can turn abstract mathematics into a useful strategy by putting these methods into practice right now.

Take into consideration the following reflection questions to broaden your understanding and relate this knowledge to your personal development. In what areas of your present AI work do you rely more on gut feeling than quantifiable proof? To what extent do you feel at ease utilizing statistics and probability to explain model errors? Which optimization choices did you make without completely comprehending how they would affect the math? How does the loss function you choose affect the moral or useful results of your system? This week, which mathematical idea from this chapter will you review and reinforce?

AI is made controllable by mathematics, not difficult. It transforms experimentation into methodical progress, complexity into structured representation, and uncertainty into measurable risk. You achieve clarity when you consciously utilize these fundamentals. You give up clarity when you ignore them. The distinction is evident in professional development, deployment success, and performance measures; it is not merely theoretical. This is where intelligent thinking starts, and it will serve as the foundation for all of your advanced capabilities.

CHAPTER IV

Machine Learning Fundamentals

Supervised Learning Overview

One of the fundamental methods in artificial intelligence and machine learning is supervised learning, which is a crucial place for novices to start when learning how to teach machines to generate predictions from data. A labeled dataset—one in which every input data point is matched with the appropriate output or target—is used to train models in supervised learning. In order for the algorithm to accurately anticipate the target for new, unseen data, it must first find a mapping from inputs to outputs. Applications where historical data with established results is available, such as classifying medical imaging, detecting spam emails, or predicting home prices based on property attributes, benefit greatly from this method. Comprehending supervised learning gives novices a foundation for handling a broad range of predictive modeling tasks and prepares them for more complex machine learning methods.

Knowing what kinds of problems supervised learning can handle is the first stage in the process. These issues are often divided into two categories: classification tasks and regression activities. Predicting continuous numerical values, such as stock prices, temperatures, or sales numbers, is the work of regression. In regression, the output variable is a numerical value, and metrics like mean squared error, mean absolute error, or R-squared scores are frequently used to assess the model's success. On the other hand, classification tasks entail making predictions about distinct categories or labels, including whether an email is spam or not, if a tumor is benign or malignant, or what kind of object is in an image.

Classification models are assessed using measures including the F1 score, recall, accuracy, and precision. Because the selection of models, preprocessing strategies, and evaluation procedures varies depending on whether the job is regression or classification, beginners benefit from understanding the differences between these problem types.

The difference between training and testing datasets is a key idea in supervised learning. Usually, the dataset is separated into two or more subsets: a testing set that is used to assess the model's performance on unknown data, and a training set that is used to train the model. To adjust hyperparameters and avoid overfitting—a phenomenon where a model performs well on training data but badly on fresh data—a third subset known as a validation set is occasionally employed. Beginners need to know how crucial it is to properly split data in order to guarantee impartial and trustworthy model evaluation. Beginners can generate reproducible training and testing partitions by using Python packages like scikit-learn, which offer routines to split datasets randomly. Creating models that perform well in real-world applications requires careful dataset management.

Two essential phases in supervised learning are feature selection and preprocessing. The quality and applicability of features, also known as input variables, have a big impact on the model's success since they give the model the data it needs to generate predictions. To increase model accuracy and computational efficiency, beginners must learn how to recognize important features and eliminate redundant or unnecessary ones. Handling missing data, converting categorical variables into numerical form, normalizing or scaling features, and creating new features by transformation or combination are examples of preprocessing procedures. By preparing the dataset in this way, discrepancies or incompatible data types won't impede the algorithm's ability to identify patterns. Because feature preprocessing has a direct impact on the performance of supervised learning models, it is an essential skill for novices to master.

In order to learn the relationship between input features and output targets, supervised learning relies on algorithms that employ labeled data. A straightforward technique for regression tasks, linear regression describes the relationship between input variables and output as a linear equation. Despite its name, logistic regression is used to predict the likelihood that a given input belongs to a specific class in binary classification problems. Decision trees, which divide data according to feature values, and ensemble techniques like random forests and gradient boosting, which combine several models to enhance predicted performance, are examples of more sophisticated algorithms. While neural networks may learn complex patterns through numerous layers of interconnected nodes, support vector machines use hyperplanes in high-dimensional space to divide classes. It is beneficial for novices to begin with simpler models, comprehend their assumptions and restrictions, and then progressively advance to more complex algorithms as their confidence and proficiency increase.

Two essential elements of supervised learning are model evaluation and performance assessment. A model's ability to generalize to new data is demonstrated by its predictions on the testing dataset after it has been trained on the training dataset. While classification models are judged on their capacity to accurately categorize instances and strike a balance between precision and recall, regression models are evaluated using metrics that quantify the difference between predicted and actual values. By splitting the dataset into several folds and training the model on distinct subsets while testing on the remaining fold, a technique known as cross-validation is frequently used to evaluate model performance more accurately. This method guarantees that outcomes are independent of a certain data split and assists novices in comprehending the diversity in model performance. Building confidence in models' predictions and choosing which models to use in real-world applications requires careful model evaluation.

Another crucial component of supervised learning that enables novices to enhance model performance is hyperparameter adjustment. The maximum depth of a decision tree, the number of neighbors in a k-nearest neighbor model, or the learning rate in gradient-based algorithms are examples of hyperparameters—external settings that affect the model's behavior. Hyperparameters need to be established before training and modified using methods like grid search or random search, in contrast to model parameters, which are learned during training. Beginners can find configurations that maximize model performance while avoiding overfitting or underfitting by experimenting with various hyperparameter settings and measuring their impact using validation datasets. Through this method, students are introduced to the iterative nature of machine learning development, where the best outcomes require constant experimentation and refinement.

Python offers a user-friendly environment for supervised learning implementation, complete with libraries and tools that streamline each step of the procedure. Because it offers ready-to-use implementations of popular algorithms, functions for splitting datasets, preprocessing tools, and ways to assess model performance, Scikit-learn is especially well-liked by novices. While visualization frameworks like matplotlib and seaborn facilitate exploratory data analysis and performance inspection, pandas and numpy enable effective data manipulation and numerical calculations. With the help of these tools, novices can create whole supervised learning processes in a single Python environment, including data preprocessing, model training, assessment, and fine-tuning.

In conclusion, supervised learning is a fundamental component of machine learning that allows models to anticipate future inputs and identify patterns in labeled data. Beginners must be able to manage training and testing datasets, choose and preprocess features, choose the right algorithms, and comprehend the difference between regression and classification jobs. Students are able to create reliable predictive models by using metrics and cross-validation to assess model performance, optimizing outcomes by adjusting hyperparameters, and utilizing Python libraries for implementation. Understanding the fundamentals of supervised learning prepares novices to take on increasingly challenging AI challenges and create useful, data-driven solutions. It also lays the groundwork for more sophisticated machine learning approaches.

Unsupervised Learning Overview

Computers can evaluate and interpret data without predetermined labels or explicit supervision thanks to unsupervised learning, a basic area of machine learning. Unsupervised learning uses raw, unannotated data to find patterns, structures, and relationships that are present in the data, as opposed to supervised learning, which trains models using datasets that contain input-output pairs. Because it lays the groundwork for data exploration, the discovery of hidden structures, and the execution of tasks like clustering, dimensionality reduction, and anomaly detection, an understanding of unsupervised learning is crucial for Python beginners. Applications requiring exploratory analysis and feature interpretation are made possible by unsupervised learning, which aims to extract valuable insights from data when the proper output is unknown.

Clustering, which entails assembling related data points according to predetermined standards or similarity metrics, is one of the main tasks in unsupervised learning. By analyzing the distances or connections between data points, clustering algorithms find patterns in the data and create groups of people who have similar traits. Beginners can experiment with techniques like k-means, hierarchical clustering, and DBSCAN thanks to Python's built-in clustering algorithms, which are provided by libraries like scikit-learn. K-means, for instance, divides the dataset into a predefined number of clusters by minimizing the variance within each group, offering a simple method of data organization. Using either agglomerative or divisive techniques, hierarchical clustering creates nested clusters that reveal links at several levels in a tree-like structure. DBSCAN works well with datasets that have irregular cluster forms since it finds clusters based on density. Beginners can identify trends and divide data for additional analysis or preprocessing by being aware of these strategies.

Another essential element of unsupervised learning that is especially helpful when dealing with high-dimensional datasets is dimensionality reduction. Many features, some of which may be unnecessary or redundant, are frequently found in real-world datasets. While maintaining the data's fundamental structure and variability, dimensionality reduction algorithms convert the data into a lower-dimensional space. A popular Python technique called principal component analysis finds orthogonal axes that capture the most variance in the data, making complex datasets easier to understand and increasing computing performance. To assist novices in exploring links and clusters in multi-dimensional data, some techniques, like t-distributed stochastic neighbor embedding, concentrate on maintaining local structures for visualization reasons. Students can enhance model performance, reduce noise, and promote a deeper comprehension of underlying patterns by lowering the number of dimensions.

Finding data points that considerably depart from the norm is known as anomaly detection, and unsupervised learning is useful for this task as well. Finding anomalies is essential in fields like banking, cybersecurity, and healthcare since they may be signs of mistakes, fraud, or uncommon but significant occurrences. Python offers tools for implementing anomaly detection through statistical methods, clustering, or specialized algorithms, enabling novices to identify anomalous data items automatically. Students who learn to identify anomalies are better equipped to deal with real-world datasets, where anomalies are frequent and can have a big impact on system reliability or decision-making.

Another crucial component of unsupervised learning is feature representation and learning. Unsupervised algorithms can generate additional features or encode the original data in ways that improve downstream model performance by looking for patterns and structures in the data. In unsupervised learning, autoencoders—a kind of neural network—compress and rebuild data into lower-dimensional representations while preserving key characteristics. These methods establish the foundation for more complex applications like deep learning and generative modeling by helping novices comprehend how algorithms can learn abstract representations without explicit supervision.

Because unsupervised learning models lack labeled outputs to directly gauge performance, evaluating them presents special difficulties. To evaluate the quality of clusters or representations, novices must instead rely on oblique metrics, visualizations, or subject expertise. Reconstruction errors gauge the precision of data approximations in dimensionality reduction techniques, whereas silhouette scores, for instance, evaluate the cohesiveness and separation of clusters. Heatmaps, dendrograms, and scatter plots are examples of visualizations that assist learners in intuitively interpreting the data, which facilitates the identification of significant patterns and the evaluation of algorithm efficacy. Gaining an understanding of evaluation in unsupervised learning allows novices to use exploratory, data-driven methods and supports the idea that insights can be obtained even in the absence of explicit labels.

Because of its adaptability, unsupervised learning can be used in a variety of real-world situations. Customers can be divided into groups according to their purchase patterns in marketing, allowing for more specialized advertising and tailored suggestions. Clustering can be used in biology to categorize species according to their characteristics or find patterns in gene expression. Anomaly detection is used in finance to find fraudulent transactions or unusual trading activity. Beginners can acquire useful abilities for identifying hidden structures in data and using analytical reasoning to solve challenging situations by studying unsupervised Python methods.

These encounters show how effective machine learning is at drawing insights from unstructured data and serve as a springboard for more sophisticated hybrid learning strategies that blend supervised and unsupervised methods.

Beginners may easily implement and experiment with unsupervised learning methods thanks to Python's library ecosystem. Libraries that facilitate preprocessing, grouping, dimensionality reduction, and result visualization include scikit-learn, NumPy, Pandas, and Matplotlib. Learners may apply various methods, examine data step-by-step, and instantly see the effects of changing parameters in interactive environments such as Jupyter Notebook. This practical method improves comprehension, boosts self-esteem, and promotes experimentation—all of which are essential for grasping the ideas and methods of unsupervised learning. Beginners can advance from theoretical understanding to real-world application by utilizing Python's tools, which enable them to identify significant patterns and insights in a variety of datasets.

To sum up, unsupervised learning is a strong and flexible method in machine learning and artificial intelligence that allows models to recognize patterns, cluster related data, lower dimensionality, spot abnormalities, and acquire meaningful representations without the need for explicit labeling. Learning the fundamentals of unsupervised learning is crucial for Python novices who want to perform exploratory data analysis, feature engineering, and data preparation for more complex modeling jobs. Finding underlying structures and relationships in data can be accomplished practically with the help of clustering, dimensionality reduction, anomaly detection, and feature learning. Python's extensive library ecosystem enables students to visualize results, test methods, and assess performance easily—all of which help to reinforce abstract ideas through practical application. Gaining knowledge in unsupervised learning gives novices the ability to evaluate unstructured data, acquire new perspectives, and use machine learning methods in a variety of contexts, laying a solid basis for future research and development in data science and artificial intelligence.

Feature Selection Techniques

A critical phase in the machine learning process, feature selection aids in enhancing interpretability, decreasing computing complexity, and improving model performance. Understanding feature selection methods is crucial for novices since a model's accuracy is directly impacted by the caliber and applicability of its input features. Repetitive or unnecessary features can cause overfitting, in which a model performs well on training data but badly on fresh, unseen data. Not all features in a dataset make a significant contribution to predictions. By identifying the key variables that best capture the underlying patterns in the data, feature selection improves the efficiency and dependability of models. Python offers a number of tools and packages, including scikit-learn, pandas, and NumPy, that make it simpler for novices to apply feature selection in real-world machine learning applications by streamlining the evaluation, selection, and transformation of features.

Filter techniques are a popular technique for feature selection that assesses each feature's significance separately from the machine learning algorithm of choice. These techniques usually rank features according to their association with the target variable using statistical measurements. Correlation coefficients can quantify the linear relationship between a feature and the goal for numerical features in regression problems. Metrics like mutual information or chi-square scores can be used to assess how dependent features are on the goal labels for categorization or classification tasks. Filter methods are a great place to start for novices since they are easy to use, computationally efficient, and offer a clear ranking of attributes. Without the need for intricate calculations, they enable learners to rapidly eliminate superfluous characteristics prior to model training, lowering dimensionality and enhancing interpretability.

Another class of feature selection strategies that assess feature subsets according to model performance is wrapper approaches. Wrapper approaches, as opposed to filter methods, evaluate how well a set of features predicts the target variable using a particular learning algorithm. A common wrapping technique is recursive feature elimination, in which features are eliminated iteratively, and the model is retrained to assess how each removal affects performance. By gradually adding or removing features, forward and backward selection strategies maximize model correctness at every stage. Wrapper methods are more computationally costly than filter methods, but they frequently produce superior results since they take feature interactions into account. Learning wrapper techniques gives novices a hands-on understanding of how various feature combinations affect predictions and how algorithm-dependent evaluation might affect the significance of a feature.

By selecting features as part of the model training process, embedded methods combine the benefits of filter and wrapper approaches. In order to achieve automatic feature selection, regularization approaches like Lasso regression add a penalty term to the loss function that incentivizes the model to set the coefficients of less significant features to zero. Algorithms based on decision trees, such as gradient boosting or random forests, assign feature relevance scores based on how each feature helps to lower error during tree construction. Workflow is streamlined by embedded approaches, which are frequently more effective than wrapper approaches and let novices choose pertinent features when training the model. Beginners can better grasp how some algorithms naturally find valuable features and how regularization can reduce overfitting while enhancing generalization by learning to use embedded approaches.

Feature selection and dimensionality reduction approaches are connected, particularly when working with high-dimensional datasets. The original characteristics are reduced to a smaller collection of uncorrelated components that account for the majority of the data variation using techniques like principal component analysis. This successfully eliminates redundancy and lowers the dimensionality of the input space without specifically choosing original features. Understanding dimensionality reduction helps beginners because it emphasizes how crucial it is to keep important information while simplifying datasets, which is especially helpful for large datasets with a lot of linked features. Learners can produce condensed, effective datasets that enhance model performance and computing speed by combining feature selection and dimensionality reduction.

Python's extensive library ecosystem enables the application of feature selection approaches to be feasible. Scikit-learn has wrappers for recursive feature removal and embedded feature importance metrics, as well as modules for filter-based selection like SelectKBest. Pandas makes it simple to compute correlation matrices and inspect data, which aids novices in seeing the connections between goal variables and characteristics. Learners can preprocess datasets, choose the best features, and feed the refined data into models by integrating these tools into machine learning pipelines, which guarantees a more efficient and organized workflow. Beginners can learn how to assess feature relevance, lower noise, and increase model performance in a variety of machine learning tasks by using these methods in Python.

Model interpretability is also significantly influenced by feature selection. Learners can gain a deeper understanding of the connections between input variables and predictions by concentrating on a subset of significant features, which also helps them comprehend how the model makes its judgments. This is especially helpful in fields where it's essential to explain model decisions, like healthcare, finance, or business analytics. Incorporating feature selection into their workflow helps novices better comprehend the data and the modeling process by teaching them how to strike a compromise between interpretability and predictive accuracy. Reducing the number of features is a crucial strategy for real-world machine learning applications because it can also reduce the danger of overfitting, speed up training, and make model maintenance easier.

To sum up, feature selection strategies are essential to creating successful machine learning models. Wrapper approaches evaluate feature subsets based on model performance, embedded methods combine feature selection with training to maximize efficiency and accuracy, and filter methods offer rapid and computationally efficient ways to evaluate the significance of individual features. These methods are enhanced by dimensionality reduction, which makes high-dimensional datasets simpler. Python provides easily usable tools for putting these strategies into practice, enabling novices to hone their feature selection abilities. Learners build the foundation required to create reliable, understandable, and effective machine learning solutions that generalize well to new data by learning to identify the most informative features, eliminate redundant or unnecessary variables, and comprehend their impact on model performance. Knowing feature selection is essential for creating useful and trustworthy AI applications; it's not merely a technical step.

Training and Validation Process

A key element of machine learning is the training and validation procedure, which enables models to learn from data and be assessed for precision and generalization. Understanding this procedure is crucial for Python newbies as it serves as the foundation for creating dependable and efficient AI systems. While validation is used to evaluate the model's performance on unseen data to make sure it generalizes well beyond the training examples, training is teaching a machine learning model to recognize patterns in a dataset by modifying its parameters to reduce errors. When combined, these procedures aid in avoiding overfitting and underfitting and direct the model architecture and hyperparameter tuning process.

Preparing a dataset, which is usually divided into at least two sections—the training set and the validation set—is the first step in the training phase. The model learns patterns and relationships from the data in the training set. Throughout the training process, the model predicts the input data, uses a loss function to compare the predictions with the actual results, and modifies its internal parameters to minimize error. Optimization algorithms like gradient descent, which calculate gradients of the loss function with respect to model parameters and iteratively update the parameters in a direction that minimizes the loss, are frequently used to carry out this adjustment process. Python novices can execute these procedures without explicitly coding the optimization by using libraries like TensorFlow, PyTorch, or scikit-learn. This way, they can concentrate on comprehending the learning process and the impact of various hyperparameters.

Since validation offers an objective assessment of a model's performance on fresh, untested data, it is essential to the training and assessment process. The model's performance is tracked at every training stage using the validation set, which is distinct from the training data. Beginners may assess if the model is learning correctly or overfitting to the training data by looking at measures like accuracy, precision, recall, or mean squared error on the validation set. When a model overfits, it memorizes the training data instead of identifying broad patterns, which leads to high accuracy on training data but subpar performance on validation or test data. Conversely, underfitting happens when the model performs poorly on both training and validation sets because it is unable to identify underlying patterns. For novices to create accurate and broadly applicable models, it is essential that they comprehend these ideas.

Cross-validation, which divides the dataset into several subgroups and trains the model on various combinations of these subsets, is a popular method to improve the efficacy of the training and validation process. In k-fold cross-validation, for instance, the dataset is split into k equal sections, and the model is trained k times, using the remaining folds as the training set and a new fold as the validation set each time. This method lowers the variance related to a single train-validation split, yielding a more reliable assessment of the model's performance. Using scikit-learn routines, novice Python programmers can do cross-validation and have practical experience evaluating the stability and performance of their models over several data partitions.

To direct model improvements, performance indicators must be tracked throughout training. Both the training and validation sets are used to monitor loss and other evaluation metrics as the model learns. Plots of training and validation loss or accuracy are used to visualize these metrics over epochs, which aids novices in understanding the dynamics of learning. Overfitting is frequently indicated by a divergence between training and validation loss, whereas underfitting is indicated by similarly high loss values. To deal with these problems, regularization strategies like L1 and L2 penalties or early stopping, which terminate training when validation performance stops getting better, are employed. With the help of these techniques, novices may efficiently optimize models, avoiding overfitting and guaranteeing adequate data learning.

Another crucial step in the training and validation process is data preprocessing. Convergence during training is enhanced by normalization, standardization, and managing missing data, which guarantee that the model receives clean and suitably scaled inputs. Effective preprocessing lowers the possibility of bias in predictions and aids in the model's ability to learn patterns. Although scikit-learn offers pipelines that combine preprocessing, training, and validation phases into a unified workflow, Python modules like Pandas and NumPy offer tools for methodically prepping and preparing data. Learning these preprocessing methods is a crucial first step for novices who want to create dependable models and comprehend the entire machine learning process.

Another element that is directly related to the training and validation procedure is hyperparameter tweaking. Hyperparameters that affect the training algorithm's behavior and the model's complexity include learning rate, batch size, number of layers, and regularization strength. Novices can find the best settings that increase model accuracy and generalization by methodically assessing performance on the validation set for various hyperparameter configurations. Python libraries offer automated tools to support popular hyperparameter tuning techniques, including grid search, random search, and Bayesian optimization. This makes it simpler for students to try out various configurations and comprehend how they affect training results.

It is customary to assess the model's performance on a different test set that was not used for either training or validation after it has been trained and validated. This last analysis offers an objective appraisal of the model's performance in practical situations. For novices, knowing the significance of the test set highlights the necessity of carefully separating datasets and reaffirms the difference between assessing generalization and learning from data. Learners create robust and efficient models that can generate trustworthy predictions on fresh data by methodically completing the training and validation process.

To sum up, the training and validation procedure is an essential starting point for Python novices studying AI and machine learning. Validation offers a way to evaluate generalization and identify overfitting or underfitting, while training enables the model to learn from data by modifying parameters to reduce mistakes. This process is improved by methods like cross-validation, data pretreatment, regularization, early halting, monitoring metrics, and hyperparameter adjustment, which guarantee accurate and dependable models. Beginners can construct, optimize, and assess machine learning models with practical skills by learning Python's training and validation methodology. This builds a strong basis for more complex AI projects and real-world applications.

Model Evaluation Methods

Model evaluation is an essential part of the machine learning process that enables novices to learn how well a model works and whether it can generalize to new, untested data. Assessing a model is essential since a model that works flawlessly on training data could not work well in real-world situations because of overfitting or inadequate generalization. In order to assess the precision, dependability, and effectiveness of predictions, the model assessment process uses particular metrics, testing plans, and validation methodologies. Building reliable machine learning systems and making sure that models produce significant and useful outcomes requires novices to become proficient in model evaluation techniques. Python has a robust library ecosystem, including scikit-learn, pandas, and NumPy, which make evaluation easier and enable students to successfully apply these techniques to a variety of models and datasets.

Splitting the dataset into distinct subsets for testing and training is the initial stage in evaluating the model. A realistic assessment of the model's predicted performance is provided by this separation, which guarantees that the model is evaluated on data that it has not seen during training. One popular method is to divide the data into two sets: one for testing, which is only used for evaluation, and another for training, which is used to understand the correlations between characteristics and targets. A validation set is another component of some workflows that is used to adjust hyperparameters and prevent overfitting. Because evaluating a model on the same data that it was trained on can produce deceptive results, beginners must grasp that effective data splitting is essential. Python tools, like scikit-learn's train_test_split function, make it simple to divide datasets in a random and repeatable manner, enabling students to test out various assessment techniques and enhancing model reliability.

Evaluation metrics for regression tasks, which entail forecasting continuous numerical values, concentrate on measuring the discrepancy between expected and actual results. R-squared score, mean squared error, and mean absolute error are examples of common metrics. Larger errors are penalized more severely by mean squared error, which computes the average squared difference between expected and actual values. In contrast, mean absolute error gives the average magnitude of errors without taking direction into account, making it a more comprehensible metric for novices. The coefficient of determination, or R-squared, calculates the percentage of the target variable's variation that the model can account for, giving information about the model's overall predictive ability. Beginners may evaluate how well their regression models are capturing patterns in the data and make well-informed judgments regarding feature selection or model improvement by being aware of these indicators.

Evaluation metrics for classification tasks, which entail categorical label prediction, center on the model's accuracy in class membership identification. The easiest statistic to understand is accuracy, which is the ratio of accurate forecasts to all instances. However, in unbalanced datasets where one class predominates, accuracy by itself can be deceptive because a model may perform well just by correctly predicting the majority class. A more sophisticated knowledge of model performance is offered by metrics like precision, recall, and F1 score. Recall calculates the percentage of true positive predictions among all real positives, whereas precision calculates the percentage of true positive forecasts across all positive predictions. The F1 score provides a balance between recall and precision by taking the harmonic mean of the two. These measures help novices understand the trade-offs between various error kinds and help them make judgments regarding threshold selection, model tweaking, and class weighting.

One popular method for more accurately evaluating model performance is cross-validation. Cross-validation separates the dataset into several folds and trains and assesses the model iteratively on several subsets rather than depending on a single train-test split. This procedure guarantees that evaluation outcomes are independent of a specific data split and lowers volatility in performance estimates. For example, K-fold cross-validation splits the dataset into k equal parts and trains on the remaining k-1 folds while utilizing each part as a test set once. This approach helps novices comprehend variability and possible overfitting by offering a thorough overview of model performance throughout the whole dataset. Because cross-validation methods are incorporated into Python libraries like scikit-learn, learners may easily implement and evaluate the findings.

By displaying the degree to which expected and actual classes match, confusion matrices offer a quantitative and visual overview of categorization performance. The matrix provides a comprehensive view of the model's mistakes by displaying counts of true positives, true negatives, false positives, and false negatives. Confusion matrices can be used by novices to spot trends in misclassification and concentrate on enhancing particular areas of model performance. For instance, reducing false negatives could be more crucial for medical diagnosis jobs than increasing total accuracy. Learners can better understand model behavior, make data-driven decisions, and effectively communicate findings when results are visualized using heatmaps or confusion matrices.

Other evaluation approaches for binary classification jobs include the area under the curve and receiver operating characteristic curves. The ROC curve shows how well the model can distinguish between classes by plotting the true positive rate against the false positive rate at various threshold levels. One numerical indicator of total discriminative power is the area under the curve. Novices learn how the model performs at different operating points and how to balance specificity and sensitivity depending on the situation. Precision-recall curves, which show how precision and recall trade off when thresholds vary, are also useful when working with imbalanced datasets.

Additionally, model evaluation encompasses specific metrics for tasks like clustering, ranking, and recommendation systems that go beyond conventional regression and classification. Metrics such as the adjusted Rand index or silhouette score are used in unsupervised learning to assess the quality of grouping in the absence of labeled data. Metrics such as normalized discounted cumulative gain or mean reciprocal rank are used in ranking or recommendation systems to evaluate how well the model arranges things based on relevance. Novices who experiment with these assessment techniques gain a flexible skill set that may be used for a variety of AI applications, such as recommendation engines and predictive modeling.

Model evaluation heavily relies on visuals in addition to quantitative measures. Beginners can immediately understand model performance by plotting anticipated versus actual values, residual plots for regression, or ROC curves for classification. Systematic errors, outliers, or trends that might be missed by numerical measures alone can be found with the use of visualization. Learners can better grasp how models function and where adjustments might be needed by combining statistical measurements with visual analysis.

To sum up, model evaluation techniques are critical to comprehending and enhancing machine learning algorithms' performance. A complete toolkit for evaluating models is provided by appropriate data splitting, cross-validation, confusion matrices, regression and classification metrics, and visualizations. These methods are accessible to novices because of Python tools like scikit-learn, pandas, and matplotlib, which enable them to apply evaluation algorithms, decipher data, and improve their models. Gaining proficiency in model evaluation enables students to create dependable, broadly applicable, and efficient machine learning systems, guaranteeing that predictions are correct and practical in real-world settings.

From Theory to Intelligent Action

This chapter is significant because it turns machine learning from a collection of technical concepts into a methodical approach to making judgments based on data. It takes more than just knowing the lingo to comprehend supervised learning, unsupervised learning, feature selection, training and validation, and model evaluation. It involves creating the conceptual framework needed to create systems that consistently learn from past experiences. Models become reliable instruments that improve judgment, automate insight, and scale decision-making when these concepts are properly implemented. Ignoring them causes initiatives to veer into conjecture, overfitting to pass for intelligence, and inaccurate forecasts to influence expensive results subtly. In the real world, the difference between a model that is meticulously trained and one that is haphazardly put together can determine whether a bank successfully prevents fraud, whether a hospital correctly identifies high-risk patients, or if a corporation makes prudent use of its resources.

Putting this chapter's lessons into practice alters your attitude to problems. You start by asking, "What kind of learning problem am I solving?" as opposed to, "Which algorithm should I use?" Rather than adding every possible variable to a model, you critically consider which aspects are actually important. You seek validation performance that demonstrates generalization rather than praising excellent training accuracy. Discipline is produced by this change. It makes you distinguish between illusion and insight and between signal and noise. Systems become brittle when their fundamentals are neglected. Models may seem accurate when they are being developed, but when they are subjected to new data, they drastically fail. Such failures are not academic in high-stakes situations; they result in monetary loss, disruption of operations, or personal injury.

Take a look at a real-world retail demand forecasting example. A business wishes to forecast the sales of its products for the next quarter. Due to the availability of historical sales data with labeled outcomes, a supervised learning strategy is used. The model becomes effective and comprehensible if the team carefully selects features, picking pertinent predictors like seasonality, pricing, promotions, and geographical trends. To guarantee generalization, the data is appropriately divided into training and validation sets during training. To evaluate performance objectively, model evaluation metrics like mean absolute error are employed. A prediction that informs inventory choices, cuts waste, and boosts profitability is the end result. The model might overfit, too, if the team omits validation or adds superfluous features like internal reference codes. Stock shortages or excess inventory will result from its failure in the upcoming quarter, despite its strong performance in previous quarters. Applying discipline makes a difference.

Machine learning can be compared to training an athlete. Similar to coaching with feedback, supervised learning involves the athlete practicing, getting feedback, and improving toward a quantifiable objective. Unsupervised learning is similar to identifying strengths and weaknesses naturally by looking for patterns in team behavior without labeling. Feature selection is the same as concentrating on the appropriate muscles and exercises rather than overtraining everything at once. Training and validation are similar to official matches versus practice games; performance needs to be evaluated in real-world scenarios. The scoreboard that establishes whether improvement is genuine is the model evaluation. The athlete may appear strong throughout training but falter under the pressure of competition if appropriate practice structure and evaluation are neglected.

This is illustrated with a brief anecdote. For a subscription business, a startup entrepreneur previously created a churn prediction model. She deployed it right away after being thrilled by preliminary results that showed 95 percent accuracy. The business discovered in a matter of weeks that the model was unable to pinpoint true churners. Since the sample was unbalanced and the majority of consumers did not churn, the high accuracy was deceptive. For almost everyone, the model has trained to anticipate "no churn." Following a review of training protocols, dataset balancing, the selection of significant behavioral characteristics, and appropriate validation, the updated model significantly increased churn detection while achieving a lower overall accuracy. Revenue leveled off. The lesson was unambiguous: evaluation must take into account genuine goals rather than flimsy criteria.

You may use a straightforward structure known as the LEARN Cycle—Label, Examine, Adjust, Review, Normalize—to make these concepts instantly effective. First, accurately label the issue. Ascertain if it is an unsupervised, supervised, or alternative paradigm. If there is a target variable, describe it. Next, look at your features. Eliminate any superfluous or unnecessary variables, and make sure the ones that remain fit the context of the issue. Third, modify your workout plan. Divide data into sets for training and validation, adjust hyperparameters methodically, and prevent leaks. Fourth, evaluate the model's performance using suitable measures that represent business objectives rather than merely practicality. Lastly, prepare the model for real-world variance and ongoing monitoring to normalize the deployment attitude. This cycle guarantees that learning systems are dynamic resources rather than static trials.

By the end of this chapter, you will be able to determine whether supervised or unsupervised learning is needed for a real-world problem and support your decision with data structure and goals. You will be able to create a feature selection approach that enhances interpretability and model performance by the end of this chapter. You will be able to put in place a training and validation procedure that guards against overfitting and data leakage by the end of this chapter. You will be able to choose and analyze assessment measures by the end of this chapter that are more in line with real-world application than with performance at the surface level.

Beyond technical endeavors, these principles have practical applications. In the corporate world, it refers to relying on solid evidence rather than just gut feeling while making judgments. It refers to the responsible enhancement of diagnostic support systems in the healthcare industry. It involves creating accountable, data-driven initiatives in public policy. It entails creating predictive tools for personal initiatives that, when faced with new data, truly function. The foundations of machine learning are precautions against false confidence, not abstract principles.

There will be inevitable repercussions if these teachings are ignored. Models grow bulky and slow when features are not chosen properly. Overfitting flourishes undetected in the absence of confirmation. In the absence of significant assessment metrics, teams optimize for the incorrect goals. Trust deteriorates with time. Data efforts lose the trust of stakeholders. Chasing little enhancements that don't provide value in the actual world wastes resources. In addition to decreasing efficiency, a lack of discipline in model building damages trustworthiness.

This chapter's main idea is encapsulated in a straightforward metaphor. It's similar to building a bridge to build a machine learning model. The goal of the bridge is defined by both supervised and unsupervised learning. The grade of materials is determined by feature selection. Structural integrity is tested during training and validation. Safety is certified by evaluation procedures. The bridge may appear complete, but collapse under load if any part is ignored. The framework facilitates mobility, development, and connection when all the components are in harmony.

As you proceed, introspection enhances comprehension. Which real-world issue in your setting would be better served by organized machine learning as opposed to ad hoc analysis? In what ways could inadequate validation skew the outcomes of a project you are working on right now? Which of the features in your current datasets are noise instead of signal? Are you selecting evaluation measures that accurately represent your goals or just those that are most straightforward to calculate? How can you use the LEARN Cycle on an actual dataset this week?

Fundamentals of machine learning are the starting point, not the end goal. Gaining proficiency with these guarantees that each subsequent advanced technique you come across will be based on solid foundations. Data becomes insight, models become tools, and predictions become meaningful action when these concepts are purposefully used.

CHAPTER V

Hands On AI Projects

Linear Regression Project

For those who are new to artificial intelligence and machine learning, a linear regression project is a great place to start because it presents fundamental ideas like evaluation metrics, data analysis, and predictive modeling in an approachable and useful way. A basic procedure called linear regression fits a linear equation to observed data in order to model the connection between a dependent variable and one or more independent variables. Starting a linear regression project gives Python novices practical experience with dataset exploration, model construction, and performance assessment, enabling them to comprehend how predictive models are created and applied in practical settings.

In a linear regression project, choosing and comprehending the dataset is the initial stage. One or more independent variables that act as predictors and a dependent variable that the model seeks to predict should both be included in the dataset. Due to their ease of use and accessibility, beginners frequently begin with basic datasets, such as those that forecast home values based on attributes like square footage, number of bedrooms, or neighborhood factors. An essential first step is data exploration, which includes variable distribution analysis, descriptive statistics, and visualization. To analyze the dataset, find patterns, correlations, and possible outliers, and get the data ready for modeling, Python libraries like Pandas, NumPy, Matplotlib, and Seaborn are frequently utilized. Beginners who comprehend the data are better able to choose features and do preprocessing, which has a direct effect on the model's performance.

Because real-world datasets frequently contain missing values, inconsistent formats, or irrelevant features, data preparation is a crucial stage in a linear regression effort. Imputation can be used to deal with missing data in two ways: either by employing predictive techniques or by substituting mean or median values for missing values. Since they cannot be employed directly in a linear regression model, categorical variables need to be numerically encoded using methods like one-hot encoding. To make sure that variables with varying units or magnitudes contribute to the model in an acceptable manner, feature scaling can also be used. Python novices can effectively preprocess data by utilizing built-in functions in libraries such as scikit-learn, which guarantee that the dataset is clean and appropriate for modeling.

Determining the link between the independent and dependent variables is a necessary step in creating the linear regression model. In its most basic form, linear regression minimizes the sum of squared errors between the predicted and actual values by fitting a line through the data points. Beginners may fit models, generate predictions, and access the coefficients and intercepts that define the line with the help of the simple LinearRegression class in Python, which is provided by the scikit-learn framework. Since these coefficients show how each independent variable contributes to the expected result, understanding them is essential. By giving students a useful understanding of how factors affect the goal, interpreting coefficients aids in the development of their technical and analytical abilities.

The evaluation phase, which comes after model construction, assesses how effectively the model forecasts fresh data. The coefficient of determination, or R-squared, mean squared error, and mean absolute error are common evaluation metrics for linear regression. These metrics measure how well predictions were made and how much of the variance in the dependent variable was due to the independent factors. Scikit-learn utilities allow Python beginners to calculate these metrics, giving them a clear picture of the model's performance. To make accurate predictions on unknown data, the model must be evaluated on a different validation set to make sure it generalizes properly and doesn't just memorize the training data.

When analyzing the outcomes of a linear regression project, visualization is essential. Learners may examine how closely the model matches the observed data by plotting the anticipated values against the actual values. The disparities between expected and actual values are shown in residual plots, which aid in spotting patterns, outliers, or heteroscedasticity that might point to model flaws or the need for more feature engineering. Python visualization modules enable novices to produce understandable and instructive charts that improve comprehension of the underlying relationships in the data and help with model interpretation.

After the model has been assessed and analyzed, novices may use regularization, polynomial regression, or feature selection to enhance performance. To cut down on noise and streamline the model, feature selection entails determining which variables are most pertinent. By incorporating higher-degree terms of independent variables, polynomial regression enables the modeling of non-linear connections. In order to avoid overfitting and enhance generalization, regularization techniques like Lasso or Ridge regression use penalty terms in the loss function. These extensions preserve the simplicity of a linear regression framework while introducing novices to increasingly complex ideas. The iterative nature of model creation is illustrated by using these techniques in Python, which also emphasizes the value of experimentation and critical thinking in machine learning projects.

Documenting results and considering the lessons learned from the data and model are often the last steps in a linear regression project. Beginners should summarize prediction performance, assess the relevance of variables, and interpret coefficients. Effectively communicating results, including significant observations, model metrics, and visuals, is a crucial ability for machine learning applications in the real world. Students get hands-on experience with the whole predictive modeling process—from data exploration and preparation to model creation, evaluation, and interpretation—by finishing a linear regression project in Python.

To sum up, a linear regression project is a fundamental exercise for Python novices learning machine learning and artificial intelligence. Important ideas like dataset exploration, preprocessing, model fitting, assessment measures, and visualization are introduced. Students gain practical skills in creating prediction models, analyzing data, and enhancing performance through iterative experimentation by finishing such a project. An easy-to-understand foundation for comprehending machine learning algorithms is provided by linear regression, and working on a practical project helps to solidify theoretical knowledge. This experience lays the foundation for future learning and success in the field of artificial intelligence by giving novices the self-assurance and technical proficiency to take on increasingly challenging machine learning projects.

Classification Project

Applying ideas and methods to real-world datasets through a classification project is a great approach for novices to get hands-on experience with machine learning. Predicting categorical labels for input data is the aim of classification, a form of supervised learning. Understanding the issue and the data is usually the first step in a classification effort. Preprocessing, model selection, training, assessment, and refinement come next. Beginners can more easily implement a full workflow and obtain practical experience in developing AI solutions thanks to Python's wide ecosystem of tools, which includes matplotlib or seaborn for data visualization, scikit-learn for machine learning methods, and pandas for data manipulation.

Data exploration is the initial stage of a classification process. To comprehend the features, goal variable, data kinds, and overall structure, beginners must look at the dataset. Examining summary statistics, spotting missing values, and displaying feature distributions are all part of exploratory data analysis. Patterns and connections between the target variable and features can be found using visualization techniques, including scatter plots, box plots, and histograms. Gaining an understanding of the data enables students to spot any issues that could affect model performance, such as outliers, imbalanced classes, or irrelevant features. In order to properly prepare the dataset for machine learning algorithms, data exploration also informs choices about feature selection and preprocessing.

A crucial phase in a classification project is data preprocessing. Missing values, irregular formatting, or categorical variables that require conversion to numerical form are common features of real-world datasets. Removing rows or columns with large gaps or imputing missing values using statistical measures like mean, median, or mode are two possible approaches to handling missing data. To make them compatible with machine learning algorithms, categorical characteristics are usually encoded using methods like label encoding or one-hot encoding. To make sure that numerical features are on the same scale, feature scaling and normalization could also be required, especially when utilizing distance-based algorithms like k-nearest neighbors. Preprocessing lowers the possibility of mistakes and enhances model performance by ensuring that the data is clean, consistent, and appropriate for modeling.

The next important step is choosing a suitable categorization algorithm. Python offers a vast array of algorithms for beginners, each with unique advantages and disadvantages. For binary classification tasks, logistic regression is a straightforward but efficient technique that yields results that are easy to understand. While ensemble techniques like random forests or gradient boosting increase accuracy by merging numerous models, decision trees are simple to visualize and produce hierarchical rules to distinguish groups. K-nearest neighbors categorize occurrences based on their resemblance to neighboring points, and support vector machines work well in high-dimensional spaces. Large datasets with non-linear relationships can benefit from the use of neural networks, which are more sophisticated models that can capture complicated patterns. The size of the dataset, its complexity, and the intended trade-off between interpretability and accuracy all influence the method choice.

The model is trained on a subset of the dataset, usually referred to as the training set, after an algorithm has been selected. By modifying internal parameters to reduce errors, the algorithm learns the link between input features and the target variable during training. Beginners need to be aware that training by itself does not ensure a high-quality model because overfitting or underfitting can happen. Underfitting arises when the model is too basic to identify patterns in the data, while overfitting happens when the model memorizes the training data and performs badly on new data. These problems are lessened by methods like cross-validation, regularization, and meticulous feature selection, which guarantee that the model performs well when applied to new data.

Assessing the model's performance after training is essential to comprehending its efficacy. Classification evaluation criteria that are frequently used include F1 score, recall, accuracy, and precision. In datasets that are unbalanced, accuracy—which quantifies the percentage of accurate predictions—can be deceptive. Recall measures the percentage of actual positives that are accurately detected, whereas precision quantifies the percentage of accurate positive forecasts. The F1 score provides a single statistic that takes into consideration both false positives and false negatives by striking a balance between precision and recall. Confusion matrices, which show the numbers of true positives, true negatives, false positives, and false negatives, are helpful tools for visualizing prediction results. Beginners can determine the advantages and disadvantages of their models and decide on future enhancements by analyzing these metrics.

In order to maximize model performance, hyperparameter adjustment is frequently required. The depth of a decision tree, the number of estimators in a random forest, or the learning rate in gradient boosting are examples of hyperparameters, which are configuration settings outside the model. Accuracy and generalization can be greatly impacted by changing these factors. Beginners can methodically investigate various hyperparameter combinations and determine the most efficient setup by using strategies like grid search or random search. A reliable solution to the classification problem is provided by models that are properly tuned and avoid overfitting or underfitting when paired with validation datasets.

Lastly, two critical components of a classification endeavor are deployment and interpretation. Predictions on fresh data can be made using the model once it performs satisfactorily. In order to comprehend how predictions are made, novices should also analyze feature importance or decision limits to explain the model's behavior. In real-world applications where it's crucial to explain model conclusions, like healthcare, finance, or business analytics, this interpretability is advantageous. Beginners receive a thorough introduction to machine learning practice by finishing a classification project, which gives them practical experience applying theoretical knowledge, preparing data, choosing and training models, assessing performance, and improving predictions.

In conclusion, by using Python to construct end-to-end workflows, a classification project provides novices with a useful framework for learning machine learning. Every stage, from data discovery and preprocessing to model selection, training, assessment, and interpretation, reaffirms fundamental ideas and methods necessary to create trustworthy AI solutions. Students who work on a categorization assignment build a solid basis for more complex machine learning and artificial intelligence applications by learning how to manage real-world data, make wise modeling decisions, and rigorously assess model performance.

Clustering Project

For novices in artificial intelligence and machine learning, a clustering project is a great method to get hands-on experience with unsupervised learning. Without the use of predetermined labels, clustering is a sort of unsupervised learning that divides data points into groups according to similarity. Because of this, it is very helpful for market segmentation, anomaly detection, exploratory data analysis, and many other practical uses. A clustering project gives Python novices a practical way to learn how algorithms may find patterns, recognize data structures, and generate insightful predictions in the absence of explicit outputs. Additionally, it exposes students to fundamental ideas, including feature preprocessing, cluster evaluation, and distance metrics.

Choosing a suitable dataset is the initial stage in a clustering effort. Multiple attributes that enable meaningful differences among data points should ideally be present in the dataset. Typical examples are sensor readings that can be grouped to identify trends or abnormalities, or customer data that includes demographics like age, income, and spending history. After selecting a dataset, novices need to investigate and comprehend it by looking at distributions, summary statistics, and feature relationships. For this stage, Python tools like Pandas, NumPy, Matplotlib, and Seaborn are very helpful since they let students examine the dataset, make visualizations, and spot possible problems like missing values, outliers, or unrelated features. Good exploration directs preprocessing choices and aids in deciding which features to include in the clustering process.

Because the quality of clusters is largely dependent on the quality of the data, data preparation is an essential phase in a clustering endeavor. Features with different sizes or units can skew findings since clustering methods rely on similarity measures, which are frequently computed using distances between data points. For instance, normalization or standardization can be necessary for a dataset that includes both age and income in order to prevent any one feature from controlling the clustering process. Incomplete data can make it impossible to calculate distance accurately, so handling missing numbers is also crucial. To ensure that the algorithm receives consistent and relevant input, beginners can use Python's preprocessing capabilities in libraries like scikit-learn to standardize features, impute missing values, and get the dataset ready for clustering.

The next step is to choose and use a clustering algorithm after the dataset is ready. Because of its ease of use and effectiveness, K-means is one of the most popular clustering methods for novices. By iteratively allocating points to the closest cluster centroid and updating centroids based on the mean of assigned points, it divides the data into a predetermined number of clusters. Another popular technique is hierarchical clustering, which uses either agglomerative or divisive techniques to produce nested clusters that enable the presentation of data linkages as dendrograms. The density-based clustering algorithm DBSCAN is very helpful for datasets with uneven cluster distributions since it can detect clusters of any shape and can deal with noise. These algorithms are implemented by Python's scikit-learn module, which enables novices to try out several approaches and see how cluster formation changes based on algorithm and parameter selections.

In clustering projects, figuring out the ideal number of clusters is crucial. While selecting too many clusters can add needless complexity to algorithms like K-means, selecting too few clusters may oversimplify the data. The number of clusters that best describe the dataset is often determined using methods like the gap statistic, silhouette analysis, and the elbow approach. To make sure that clusters are compact inside and well-separated outside, these techniques focus on assessing metrics of cluster cohesiveness and separation. These methods can be used by novices in Python to understand the structure of their data and choose the right number of clusters, which has a direct impact on the results' interpretability and use.

Another crucial element of a clustering effort, especially for novices, is visualizing clusters. With the help of visualizations, students can quickly comprehend how the algorithm has arranged the data points and spot trends or abnormalities that would not be immediately apparent from numerical results alone. While dimensionality reduction methods like principal component analysis or t-distributed stochastic neighbor embedding can project higher-dimensional data into two or three dimensions for visualization, scatter plots, which are colored by cluster assignments, are frequently used for two-dimensional datasets. These visualizations may be easily created with Python packages such as Matplotlib and Seaborn, which offer instant feedback on clustering findings and assist novices in interpreting and improving their models.

Because unsupervised learning lacks specified labels, evaluating clustering results poses special obstacles. Internal evaluation metrics that quantify cluster quality by evaluating cohesiveness, separation, and compactness include silhouette scores, Davies-Bouldin index, and inertia. When ground truth labels are provided for comparison using measures like the adjusted Rand index or normalized mutual information, external evaluation might be feasible. Python novices can use these metrics to evaluate cluster quality, compare various methods, and improve preprocessing or parameter selections, gaining a better grasp of how algorithm settings and data properties affect clustering outcomes.

Lastly, the findings of a clustering endeavor are often interpreted and used. In order to spot trends, group behaviors, or odd patterns, learners might examine the features of each cluster. For instance, clusters may indicate various purchasing patterns in a client segmentation project, allowing for more focused marketing tactics. Clusters can identify anomalies and show common operational patterns in sensor or network data. Beginners acquire experience in both technical implementation and converting data-driven results into useful information by recording findings, displaying clusters, and summarizing ideas.

To sum up, a clustering project offers novices a thorough introduction to Python unsupervised learning. Dataset selection, exploration, preprocessing, algorithm selection, cluster evaluation, visualization, and interpretation are among the crucial tasks that are covered. Students get hands-on experience in seeing patterns in unlabeled data, comprehending algorithm behavior, and using assessment tools to gauge model quality by working through a clustering project. Python's extensive library ecosystem makes implementation easier, freeing up novices to concentrate on analysis and experimentation. After finishing a clustering assignment, students are better prepared to handle real-world data issues, derive insightful conclusions, and lay the groundwork for more complex unsupervised learning and machine learning initiatives.

Text Analysis Project

For novices, a text analysis project is the perfect method to investigate how machine learning and artificial intelligence may be used to process and comprehend unstructured data. The process of collecting significant information from text, seeing patterns, and drawing conclusions that can guide choices or forecasts is called text analysis, sometimes referred to as natural language processing. Python offers a plethora of tools and libraries, like scikit-learn for machine learning models, NLTK and spaCy for natural language processing, matplotlib or seaborn for visualization, and pandas for data handling. Beginners can get hands-on experience handling real-world data, cleaning and manipulating textual information, and using machine learning techniques to extract useful insights from written content by working on a text analysis project.

Understanding the dataset and the issue that has to be resolved is the first stage in every text analysis effort. Text datasets can take many different forms, such as emails, transcripts, news articles, product reviews, and social media posts. In order to identify the text fields and any related labels or metadata, such as categories, ratings, or timestamps, beginners must look at the dataset's structure. Exploratory data analysis involves reviewing summary statistics, such as the number of documents, the average length of text, or the frequency of missing values. Word frequency or phrase visualization can also offer preliminary insights into the dataset, assisting students in comprehending the information distribution and identifying irregularities. In order to guarantee that the dataset is prepared for analysis, this preliminary investigation directs later preprocessing and feature engineering procedures.

An essential part of every text analysis effort is data preprocessing. Punctuation, special characters, digits, and irregular capitalization are all common features of sloppy raw text. Beginners need to learn how to systematically clean the data, which includes standardizing formats, changing text to lowercase, and eliminating extraneous letters. For additional analysis, tokenization—the process of dividing text into discrete words or significant units—is crucial. Lemmatization and stemming assist in breaking down words into their most basic forms so that different variants of the same word are handled uniformly. Common words that have little significance, such as "the," "and," or "is," are called stop words. They may be eliminated to cut down on noise. Beginners who are proficient in preprocessing get the text data ready for feature extraction and machine learning models.

For machine learning algorithms to process textual data efficiently, it must be converted into numerical representations. Word occurrences or their relative importance in the dataset are captured by converting text into vectors using techniques like bag-of-words or term frequency-inverse document frequency. More sophisticated embeddings, like Word2Vec or GloVe, capture contextual information by encoding semantic links between words into continuous vectors. Learning a variety of representation strategies is beneficial for beginners because they offer varying degrees of performance and detail based on the project's goals. Accurate classification, sentiment analysis, or clustering are made possible by the machine learning model's ability to recognize patterns and correlations in the text, thanks to proper feature extraction.

The kind of problem being tackled in the text analysis project determines which machine learning model is best. Algorithms like logistic regression, naive Bayes, support vector machines, or random forests are frequently used for classification tasks like spam detection, sentiment analysis, or subject categorization. Unsupervised learning techniques like k-means or hierarchical clustering are suitable for clustering tasks like detecting themes or putting similar documents together. Sequence-based models, including recurrent neural networks or transformers, are powerful for tasks like language translation or text generation. To ensure a firm grasp of how each algorithm handles textual data, beginners should begin with simpler models to grasp the basics and then progressively experiment with more intricate architectures as their abilities advance.

An essential part of every text analysis effort is assessing the model's performance. Metrics like accuracy, precision, recall, and F1 score are frequently used to evaluate how effectively a model predicts categories or labels for supervised tasks. Confusion matrices show the model's weak points and offer a visual representation of classification results. Metrics such as cluster purity or silhouette score are useful for assessing the caliber of clustering outcomes for unsupervised tasks. Visualizing predictions or cluster assignments also helps beginners understand the results more easily. A thorough evaluation guarantees that the model works well with unknown data and enables students to pinpoint areas that require more preprocessing, feature engineering, or model tuning.

For a text analysis project to operate at its best, hyperparameter adjustment and model refinement are frequently required. A model's ability to learn from data is influenced by hyperparameters like regularization strength, feature count, and tree depth, which can have a big impact on accuracy and generalization. By using strategies like grid search or random search, students can methodically try out several configurations and choose the one that yields the greatest results. Model performance can also be increased by repeatedly improving preprocessing procedures, choosing pertinent features, or modifying vectorization techniques. By using these refinement strategies, novices gain the ability to improve machine learning workflows and create reliable, practical models for real-world applications.

Lastly, two crucial consequences of a text analysis project are deploying models and analyzing data. Gaining knowledge about which characteristics or terms influence forecasts the most enhances interpretability and sheds light on the linkages within the data. This is especially helpful in fields where clear communication of actionable insights is required, such as sentiment monitoring, content moderation, and customer feedback analysis. A model can be used to handle fresh text input, automate processes, or aid in decision-making once it performs well enough. Beginners can gain practical experience in managing unstructured data, implementing machine learning algorithms, assessing performance, and extracting insights by completing a text analysis project. This gives them a thorough introduction to real-world applications of artificial intelligence and natural language processing.

In conclusion, a text analysis project provides novices with an organized and useful way to study machine learning using actual data. Every stage, from preprocessing and dataset exploration to feature extraction, model selection, assessment, and improvement, strengthens essential abilities for working with textual data. Python's libraries facilitate the implementation of each project step, allowing students to create precise and understandable models. Beginners may tackle increasingly complicated AI problems and extract valuable insights from unstructured text data by finishing a text analysis project, which gives them a strong foundation in natural language processing, supervised and unsupervised learning, and model evaluation.

Image Recognition Project

Beginners may apply machine learning techniques to real-world situations in an entertaining and useful way with an image recognition project. A fundamental problem in artificial intelligence, image recognition is teaching a computer to recognize objects, patterns, or features within images. Its applications range from facial identification and medical imaging to driverless cars. Working on an image recognition project introduces basic ideas of computer vision, neural networks, and feature extraction while giving Python novices practical experience with data preprocessing, model creation, and evaluation. It improves both technical proficiency and conceptual comprehension by enabling students to relate theoretical knowledge to real-world applications.

Choosing an appropriate dataset is the first step in an image recognition project. From straightforward sets of handwritten numbers, like the MNIST dataset, to more intricate datasets with images of objects or animals, datasets can take many different forms. Designing the project requires an understanding of the dataset's properties because preprocessing choices and model complexity are influenced by elements such as image size, color channels, and class balance. Python modules like NumPy, Pandas, and Matplotlib are helpful for viewing sample images, examining class distributions, and evaluating datasets. Beginners can learn about the difficulties in picture recognition, such as changes in lighting, orientation, and background noise, by examining the data. These issues must be resolved in order to increase model accuracy.

An essential step in getting pictures ready for analysis is data preparation. Inconsistencies in size, format, or color representation are frequently seen in raw photos. While normalizing pixel values or turning photographs to grayscale might lower computational complexity and increase learning efficiency, resizing images to a uniform dimension guarantees that the input to the model is consistent. Rotation, flipping, scaling, and other image augmentation techniques broaden the variety of training data and aid in avoiding overfitting. Beginners may prepare huge datasets with minimal human labor thanks to Python modules like OpenCV, Pillow, and Keras, which offer tools to carry out these preprocessing procedures effectively. Effective preprocessing guarantees that the model won't be sidetracked by unimportant input fluctuations and can concentrate on discovering significant patterns.

The next stage is to build the model, and novices frequently begin with rudimentary neural networks or machine learning techniques. The ability of convolutional neural networks, or CNNs, to automatically identify hierarchical patterns in images, such as edges, textures, and forms, makes them very useful for image identification. In order to extract and classify features, a CNN usually includes several convolutional layers, pooling layers, and fully connected layers. CNN implementation is made easier by Python frameworks like TensorFlow and PyTorch, which include prebuilt layers, activation functions, and optimization algorithms that make it simple for novices to build, train, and assess models. Learners can better understand the basic ideas of deep learning for computer vision by comprehending how fully connected layers classify images and how convolutional layers extract features.

Labeled images from the dataset are fed into the model during training, and its parameters are changed to minimize a loss function that measures the discrepancy between the labels that were predicted and those that were actually applied. To assess their development, beginners monitor performance indicators like accuracy, precision, and recall, and employ optimization algorithms like gradient descent. To ensure that the model works effectively on unseen photos, validation sets are employed to keep an eye on generalization and avoid overfitting. Learners can gain insight into learning dynamics and comprehend how performance is impacted by hyperparameters like learning rate or batch size by visualizing training and validation accuracy over epochs. These monitoring strategies are simple to apply with Python tools, enabling novices to iterate and improve their models efficiently.

Testing the finished model on a different collection of photos allows you to gauge its effectiveness and pinpoint areas that need work. Visual examinations of predicted versus real images, classification reports, and confusion matrices offer information on how well the model differentiates between classes. In order to comprehend error patterns, such as misclassifying similar objects or failing in low light, beginners can recognize misclassified photos. This assessment highlights the significance of both model design and data quality while assisting students in understanding the difficulties associated with picture recognition.

Opportunities to investigate improvements like transfer learning, which uses pretrained models as a foundation to exploit knowledge gathered from huge datasets, are also presented by image recognition projects. With smaller datasets and less processing power, novices can get greater accuracy through transfer learning. Through libraries like Keras and PyTorch, Python gives users access to a large number of pretrained models, allowing students to experiment with more complex methods while comprehending how feature extraction and fine-tuning actually operate.

Finally, an image recognition project offers a hands-on introduction to computer vision, neural networks, and machine learning for Python beginners. It introduces ideas like convolutional layers, loss functions, and transfer learning while going over crucial procedures, including dataset selection, preprocessing, model development, training, validation, and evaluation. Students who complete such a project acquire practical experience, hone their critical thinking abilities, and comprehend how abstract ideas are translated into practical image-based tasks. In the process of acquiring machine learning and artificial intelligence, completing an image recognition project gives novices the fundamental abilities they need to take on increasingly complex AI applications, such as autonomous systems and medical diagnostics.

From Theory to Tangible Impact

This chapter is important because it turns artificial intelligence from a theoretical idea into something you can construct, test, and improve yourself. Theoretically, many people comprehend AI, but they never go beyond reading explanations or watching tutorials. Experience distinguishes active capabilities from passive comprehension. You go from being a consumer of AI information to a creator when you finish practical tasks. That transformation alters your self-esteem, professional prospects, and problem-solving skills. Applying what you've learned from these projects can help you spot data patterns, organize disorganized information, and identify opportunities where others perceive complication. Your knowledge will remain brittle if you overlook this application phase. Without action, ideas wilt, hesitancy increases, and chances are lost. When you can confidently state, "I know how to approach this with AI," in response to a company problem, community challenge, or personal endeavor, you are making a real-life effect.

Practically speaking, this chapter's experiments show that AI is not just for big tech firms. Linear regression demonstrates how historical data may be used to model patterns and generate forecasts. Classification shows how systems may identify patterns to make judgments. Hidden groupings in data that were not initially apparent are revealed by clustering. Machines can now decipher human language through text analysis, transforming reviews, comments, and feedback into useful information. Systems can understand visual information, such as identifying objects or spotting flaws, thanks to image recognition. When taken as a whole, these initiatives demonstrate that AI is a toolkit for resolving a variety of practical issues. When used regularly, these technologies speed up decision-making, lower human error, and reveal hidden insights.

Think about a real-world example. Consider a proprietor of a small retail company who wishes to boost monthly sales. She forecasts demand based on seasonal patterns using regression. She uses classification to determine which clients are most likely to react favorably to promotions. She uses clustering to divide her clientele into relevant groups according to their purchasing patterns. She uses text analysis to find common problems in consumer evaluations. She uses image recognition to automatically assess the quality of product photos that are posted to her online store. What started out as conjecture turns into a data-driven approach. Increased revenue is the result of planned experimentation and well-informed action, not chance. This is the effect of using practical AI skills in the actual world.

You can utilize the BUILD framework to put what you've learned to use right away: Start with a well-defined problem, comprehend the data, apply an appropriate model, gain insight from assessment metrics, and then deploy or iterate. First, state the issue in quantifiable words. Second, collect and examine pertinent data while looking for biases, gaps, and patterns. Third, depending on the nature of the problem, choose and apply the proper algorithm. Fourth, assess performance by examining both strengths and deficiencies using precise measures. Lastly, implement the solution in a limited setting and make adjustments in response to feedback. This methodical technique guarantees consistent growth and avoids overwhelm.

Hands-on AI initiatives can be compared to learning to drive instead of just reading a traffic manual. You can commit every traffic sign and regulation to memory, but you won't be really ready for the road until you get behind the wheel, adjust your mirrors, and put the pedal down. Projects serve as a learning experience where errors are turned into lessons rather than catastrophes. They improve judgment, flexibility, and reflexes. Your knowledge is theoretical and brittle without them. It becomes automatic and dependable with them.

This change is demonstrated with a brief narrative. Marco, a young analyst, studied AI principles online for months.

Real datasets terrified him, even though he grasped terminology and formulas. He initially hesitated when he ultimately made the decision to develop a basic classification model for forecasting client attrition at his business. The results were not perfect, and the data were disorganized. Rather than give up, he repeated. He experimented with evaluation measures, cleansed the data, and changed parameters. His model finally reached a significant level of accuracy after multiple trials. When Marco's manager saw how his reporting insights had improved, he became more confident and well-known. The choice to use what was learned in a concrete endeavor was the pivotal moment, not a new course or book. That choice changed his course.

Applying this chapter helps you build resilience in problem-solving. You gain knowledge about optimizing, refining, and debugging. You realize that flawed outcomes are not evidence of failure but rather a necessary component of the process. Additionally, you acquire a portfolio of work that shows your abilities rather than merely your academic understanding. If you ignore it, you run the risk of developing a conceptual understanding of AI but being hesitant when actual data is presented. The value of demonstrated skill is growing. Credibility is increased by application.

Impact in real life goes beyond advancing one's career. AI projects can boost academic research, maximize individual productivity, streamline nonprofit operations, and promote community efforts. For instance, community organizers can find underserved populations by using clustering algorithms. Text analysis can be used to summarize resident input. Resource requirements can be predicted by regression models. Environmental monitoring can benefit from image recognition. These are direct applications of the abilities mastered in this chapter, not far-off possibilities.

You will be able to identify a real-world issue and match it with a suitable AI solution by the end of this chapter. You will be confident in your ability to prepare and study datasets by the end of this chapter. You will be able to apply and assess text, image, regression, classification, and clustering models by the end of this chapter. You will be able to improve a model at the conclusion of this chapter using feedback and performance measurements. You will be able to create a tiny, deployable AI solution that meets a real-world demand by the end of this chapter.

Use the PRACTICE loop, a straightforward, step-by-step procedure, to put these abilities to use right away: Choose a minor, actual issue, Examine the data at hand, use an appropriate model, Analyze outcomes versus expectations, adjust parameters and clean data, put improvements into practice, effectively communicate findings, and grow gradually. Action is prioritized over perfection in this loop. Begin modestly. Finish one complete cycle. Then get better.

Here, the analogy of a workshop is helpful. Knowledge can be compared to a well-organized set of tools on a wall. Until you pick them up and construct something, they are useless, despite their magnificent appearance. Hands-on projects include building furniture out of raw materials. The initial component might sway. The second is preferable. Your craftsmanship becomes better with time. AI functions similarly. Every project improves your technical accuracy and insight.

To strengthen your application and dedication, consider the following questions as you proceed. Which actual issue in your community or place of employment could be resolved with one of the AI techniques used here? What preconceptions or anxieties have prevented you from carrying out a project? What kind of project did you find easiest to understand, and how can you improve on that?

What specific metrics will you use to assess the results of your upcoming AI experiment? In the next seven days, what modest project can you start?

This chapter serves as a starting point rather than a destination. The real value is in continuing to develop, test, and improve solutions outside of the page, not in finishing tasks. Applying practical AI abilities on a regular basis allows you to do more than examine data. You take complexity and turn it into clarity, uncertainty into direction, and information into opportunity. The true potential of useful artificial intelligence lies in that change.

CHAPTER VI

AI Workflow and Deployment

Problem Definition Strategy

One of the most important and first tasks in any machine learning or artificial intelligence project is problem definition. In order to guarantee that the efforts made in data collection, model creation, and evaluation are in line with the intended results, a precise problem definition gives guidance, defines expectations, and specifies the success criteria. Because it establishes the framework for all other processes in the machine learning workflow, it is crucial for novices to comprehend the significance of problem specification. Projects may become misdirected, ineffective, or yield unactionable outcomes if the problem is not clearly stated. In order to build and implement successful AI solutions, a strong problem definition method entails comprehending the context, defining goals, defining the problem type, and establishing limitations and assessment metrics.

Understanding the context in which the problem exists is the first step in defining the problem. In order to use the model or profit from its results, beginners must investigate the field, get background data, and determine the stakeholders. This stage frequently necessitates talking with subject-matter specialists, reading pertinent literature, and comprehending the environment's realistic limitations and challenges. For instance, knowledge of customer behavior, corporate objectives, and available data sources is necessary for a project that aims to forecast client attrition in a business setting. Beginners can make sure that the issue they are tackling is pertinent, significant, and in line with real-world requirements by thoroughly understanding the context.

This is essential for creating solutions that offer actual value.

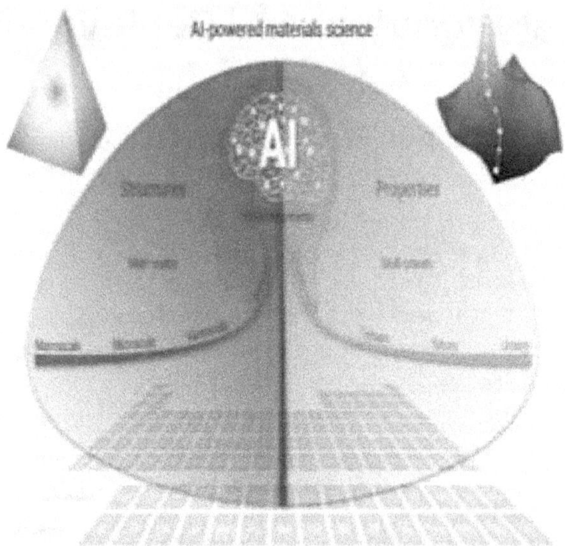

The next stage is to clearly state the project's goals after the background has been established. Whether it is forecasting numerical values, categorizing objects, or identifying anomalies, objectives specify what the machine learning model is supposed to accomplish. Beginners can choose the best algorithms, set evaluation criteria, and concentrate on the right tasks with the support of clear objectives. For example, the goal must indicate if the model's objective is to maximize accuracy, minimize false negatives, or optimize the balance between precision and recall if the objective is to detect fraudulent transactions. Beginners can track their progress, measure the model's success objectively, and make well-informed judgments about trade-offs during development by establishing clear goals.

A successful implementation also depends on properly framing the issue. The three main categories of machine learning problems—supervised learning, unsupervised learning, and reinforcement learning—each call for distinct strategies, algorithms, and assessment techniques. Predicting results using labeled data, such as sales numbers or spam email detection, is known as supervised learning. Finding patterns or structures in unlabeled data, like customer segmentation or grouping related documents together, is the main goal of unsupervised learning. In robotics or game strategies, for example, reinforcement learning entails teaching agents to make successive choices in order to maximize cumulative rewards. Because it influences the selection of models, data needs, and assessment techniques, beginners must specify the kind of problem they are attempting to solve. Proper problem framing guarantees the project's smooth progress and prevents needless complexity or goal misalignment.

Defining limits and assumptions is a crucial part of problem definition. Limitations on time, computational resources, data availability, and ethical considerations are a few examples of constraints. For example, real-time applications could have latency or performance constraints, and some datasets might contain sensitive information that needs to be compliant with privacy laws. Model selection and preprocessing procedures are guided by assumptions, such as the predicted distribution of data or the independence of characteristics. Setting reasonable expectations, avoiding potential hazards, and devising risk-reduction plans are all made easier for novices when limitations and assumptions are expressed clearly. This stage also emphasizes how crucial it is to take into account real-world aspects that influence the viability and relevance of AI solutions outside of theoretical models.

Since evaluation metrics define how success is measured and direct model optimization, they are a crucial component of problem conceptualization. Novices should choose metrics that take into account the context of the problem and match the project's goals. While classification tasks may depend on accuracy, precision, recall, or F1 scores, regression tasks typically employ measures like mean squared error or mean absolute error. Metrics such as precision-recall curves or the area under the receiver operating characteristic curve offer a more nuanced picture of model performance in unbalanced datasets. An early definition of assessment criteria guarantees that the model is built to maximize pertinent results and that advancement can be methodically evaluated. Additionally, it assists novices in objectively evaluating various strategies and determining which one best suits the current issue.

Determining the problem also entails organizing the data strategy and procedure. Since the quality and structure of data have a big impact on model performance, beginners should think about the need for data collecting, cleaning, and preprocessing. The technique for creating data that appropriately reflects the problem domain includes identifying important features, dealing with missing values, and guaranteeing consistency. During this planning stage, possible problems like noisy data, outliers, or missing labels are anticipated, and solutions are designed. In order to minimize errors and inefficiencies during implementation, a thorough problem definition strategy guarantees that data preparation and model creation are in line with the project objectives.

Lastly, a clear problem statement aids stakeholders in understanding the goal and extent of the project. Collaboration, feedback, and team member alignment are all made possible by well-documented problems, objectives, assumptions, limitations, and evaluation criteria. Beginners can develop their critical thinking and project management abilities by practicing the creation of clear problem statements, which will equip them to approach machine learning projects methodically. It also creates a benchmark for evaluating the usefulness of the finished model, defending choices, and gauging progress.

To sum up, the cornerstone of any successful machine learning project is a problem description strategy. Essential steps include comprehending the context, clearly stating the goals, identifying the limitations and assumptions, framing the problem type, establishing assessment criteria, organizing the workflow, and outlining the project's purpose. Understanding problem definition gives novices emphasis, direction, and a methodical way to apply AI solutions. By taking the effort to define the problem precisely, students make sure that their models meet real-world requirements, function well, and provide useful insights—laying a solid basis for real-world machine learning activity.

Data Collection Planning

One of the most important phases of any artificial intelligence and machine learning project is data collection planning, especially for novices learning Python through an organized curriculum. Many students are excited to start creating models and experimenting with algorithms right away. Still, seasoned professionals know that the caliber and applicability of the data used to train any machine learning system are critical to its success. Time is saved, mistakes are decreased, and the outcomes are more reliable when careful planning is done at the start. In a step-by-step learning process, knowing how to arrange data-collection aids effectively helps novices form professional and disciplined habits that will benefit them throughout their careers.

Clearly describing the problem is the first stage in planning for data collection. It is impossible to determine what information should be gathered in the absence of a clear aim. An ambiguous objective like "analyze customer behavior" is insufficient. Rather, the issue needs to be reframed as a specific topic, such as identifying which clients are most likely to discontinue using a service or projecting future sales based on historical patterns. Determining the desired result helps identify the necessary input features. This level teaches novices using Python for machine learning how to relate quantifiable data points to real-world problems. It guarantees that each piece of information gathered serves a specific function.

Finding the right data sources becomes the next priority after the goal has been established. Data may originate from internet sources, surveys, sensors, application programming interfaces, internal firm databases, or manually documented observations. Every source has its own advantages and disadvantages. Because they are readily available and ready to use, public datasets are frequently practical for novices. They may not be a perfect fit for a particular company issue. Internal data might be more pertinent, but it might need more cleaning and authorization. Planning entails determining if the selected sources are trustworthy, current, and indicative of the issue under study. This thorough assessment avoids using skewed or unnecessary data.

Determining the kind and structure of data needed is a crucial part of planning. Numerical values, category data, text, pictures, audio, and time-based records can all be used in machine learning applications. While unstructured data, like text or graphics, adds complexity, structured data in tables is typically simpler for novices to manage. By preparing ahead of time, students can select appropriate tools and anticipate preprocessing steps. It also aids in estimating computing and storage needs. Beginners can steer clear of potential technical issues later in the workflow by taking format and structure into account early on.

Another aspect that needs careful consideration is the quantity of the data. Overfitting, a problem where models recall patterns instead of learning broad trends, can result from having too little data. However, gathering too much data without enough storage or processing capacity can impede advancement. When using personal computers, novices need to be aware of their limits. Estimating the amount of data required to get significant outcomes while adhering to resource constraints is part of planning. Gaining practical machine learning skills includes understanding this equilibrium.

A key component of successful projects is high-quality data. If a dataset has errors, missing values, duplication, or inconsistencies, it can still yield subpar results, regardless of its size. It's critical to foresee possible quality problems and create solutions for them throughout the planning phase. This could entail establishing protocols for dealing with missing data, standardizing data formats, or establishing validation rules. Beginners should understand that data validation and cleaning are essential steps in the process, not an afterthought. The model is trained on accurate data thanks to a carefully thought-out quality assurance approach.

Planning for data collection also requires careful consideration of ethical issues. Transparency, equity, and privacy must all be respected while using data responsibly. Appropriate consent and data protection procedures must be followed if personal data is being gathered. Planning should cover who will have access to sensitive data and how it will be safely stored. Potential biases in the data should also be taken into consideration. The model's projections could be unjust or erroneous if some groups are underrepresented. Early in their educational path, novices should become conscious of these ethical obligations.

Another area that benefits from thorough planning is the sampling strategy. It is frequently impractical to get data from a whole population. Rather, a representative sample needs to be chosen. Developing an impartial and equitable sampling strategy contributes to the dataset's accurate representation of the general population. While stratified techniques guarantee that significant subgroups are included, random sampling lessens systematic bias. Even a technically sound model may not work in practical settings without enough sampling.

In tasks involving supervised learning, labeling is particularly crucial. Labeled examples are essential for training models that categorize or forecast results. Choosing how labels will be created and validated should be part of the planning process. While automatic labeling methods need to be reviewed for faults, human annotation may need explicit standards to ensure uniformity. Establishing quality control measures during planning enhances reliability because incorrect labels have a direct impact on model performance.

Another important factor is how to arrange and store the data that has been gathered. Clear naming conventions, documentation, and consistent formats should all be used when storing data. Analysis and upcoming improvements are made easier with well-organized storage. Additionally, reproducibility is supported by keeping track of the methods and dates of data collection. Early adoption of sound organizing techniques will make it simpler for novices to oversee and communicate their initiatives.

The planning process is further shaped by time and resource management. Data collection may need continuous monitoring, technical setup, or collaboration with others. Realistic deadlines help avoid hasty judgments that degrade quality. The project's viability is maintained by taking storage capacity, hardware constraints, and possible expenses into account.

Data collection planning is the cornerstone of the entire machine learning workflow in a progressive Python learning architecture, not just a preparatory step.

Beginners build a solid foundation for successful analysis by establishing clear goals, choosing trustworthy sources, figuring out the types and volume of data, guaranteeing quality and ethics, creating equitable sample techniques, arranging storage, developing labeling procedures, and managing resources. Data can be transformed from a random collection of facts into a structured and valuable asset with careful planning. Learners position themselves for more accurate models, more efficient processes, and increased confidence in their machine learning journey when they approach this stage with consideration.

Model Deployment Techniques

Making a trained model usable by enabling it to make predictions on fresh, real-world data is known as model deployment, and it is a crucial stage in the machine learning lifecycle. Understanding deployment strategies is crucial for novices since creating an accurate model is not enough; in order to be used in real-world applications, the model must also be dependable, efficient, and accessible. Businesses, academics, and developers may use artificial intelligence for decision-making, automation, and real-time analytics thanks to deployment, which closes the gap between model development and actionable findings. Beginners can move from experimental to production with Python's robust ecosystem of tools, frameworks, and libraries that streamline the deployment process.

A model must go through a thorough examination and validation process prior to deployment in order to guarantee that it operates dependably on unknown data. In order to confirm accuracy, robustness, and generalizability, this stage entails evaluating the model using holdout datasets, cross-validation findings, and real-world instances. Novices should be aware that even if a model performs exceptionally well on training data, it may not work well in production if it has overfitted or if the new input data is very different from the training data. Model versioning, edge case testing, and prediction performance monitoring are among the strategies that assist in reducing these risks and guarantee that the deployed model continues to function as intended. Long-term usability and successful implementation are predicated on a well-validated model.

Web APIs are a popular method for deploying models since they let apps contribute data to the model and get real-time predictions. Python frameworks like Flask and FastAPI offer simple ways to incorporate machine learning models into RESTful APIs. End customers can now access forecasts thanks to this method's interaction with online apps, mobile apps, and other services. Deploying models as APIs helps novices because it shows how their work can be used in real-world scenarios and teaches fundamental software engineering topics like server management, request handling, and response formatting. Deploying web APIs works especially well for applications like chatbots, recommendation engines, and fraud detection technologies that need to make predictions instantly.

Another popular deployment method that improves scalability, portability, and reproducibility is containerization. In order to guarantee consistent behavior across several systems, developers can package the model, dependencies, and runtime environment into a single container using tools like Docker. Containerization reduces compatibility problems and promotes teamwork by streamlining deployment on local servers, cloud platforms, or edge devices. Learning to containerize models gives novices useful experience with orchestration, environment management, and version control, among other contemporary software deployment techniques. When cloud services or microservices architectures are combined with containerization, models can effectively serve a large number of users while retaining flexibility and dependability.

Because of its scalability and accessibility, cloud deployment has grown in popularity. By offering managed services for deploying machine learning models, platforms like AWS, Google Cloud Platform, and Microsoft Azure allow novices to host models without requiring in-depth infrastructure knowledge. Benefits of cloud deployment include monitoring, automatic scaling, and interaction with data pipelines, which facilitate model management in production. Models can be deployed as endpoints, integrated with dashboards or web apps, and performance can be tracked in real time by anyone using cloud services. For students who want to implement AI solutions at scale and make models available to a wider audience, it is imperative that they comprehend cloud deployment strategies.

Another deployment method that works well in situations when real-time forecasts are not necessary is batch processing. Batch deployment generates predictions for the full dataset at once when data is gathered over time and analyzed in bulk. For jobs like creating monthly sales projections, evaluating huge datasets, or creating recurring reports, this method works well. While workflow automation systems like Apache Airflow or Luigi can schedule and manage prediction pipelines, Python modules like pandas and NumPy make batch processing easier. Batch deployment helps novices learn how to effectively manage massive data sets, maximize computation, and incorporate models into daily tasks without requiring continual human involvement.

In order to guarantee continuous performance and dependability, monitoring and maintenance are essential elements of model deployment. A model's prediction quality may be impacted by environmental conditions, shifting user behavior, or shifting data distributions after it is put into use. In order to enable prompt interventions when performance deteriorates, novices should learn how to use monitoring systems that track parameters like accuracy, response time, and error rates. Accuracy and relevance are preserved throughout time with the use of strategies like recording forecasts, monitoring data drift, and retraining models using updated datasets. Good monitoring teaches novices the value of continuous review after first deployment and supports the iterative nature of machine learning initiatives.

When deploying, security and accessibility considerations are also crucial. Models that are implemented as cloud platforms or APIs need to be secured against malicious inputs, illegal access, and data breaches. While preserving usability for authorized users, techniques like rate limitation, input validation, encryption, and authentication aid in securing deployed models. The ethical and legal ramifications of using AI models should also be taken into account by novices, especially when managing sensitive data, maintaining equity, and avoiding unforeseen outcomes. By addressing these issues, students are better equipped to use models properly in practical settings.

To sum up, model deployment strategies allow machine learning models to go from experimental prototypes to workable solutions that produce tangible benefits. Beginners have a variety of options for making models scalable, dependable, and accessible thanks to techniques like online APIs, containerization, cloud deployment, batch processing, monitoring, and security precautions. Gaining an understanding of deployment gives students the ability to incorporate AI into applications, sustain performance over time, and handle real-world problems in production settings. Beginners can finish the entire machine learning lifecycle by becoming proficient in deployment tactics, turning models into workable systems that provide useful insights and address actual issues.

Performance Monitoring

A crucial part of the machine learning lifecycle is performance monitoring, which ensures models remain accurate, reliable, and applicable over time. Understanding performance monitoring is crucial for Python beginners learning artificial intelligence and machine learning, since creating a model is just the first step; maintaining and assessing its efficacy in real-world scenarios is just as crucial. Changes in data distribution, operating conditions, or user behavior cause a model that performs well at first to deteriorate without adequate monitoring, resulting in inaccurate predictions, decreased performance, and potentially expensive errors. Tracking important indicators, spotting indications of model deterioration, examining mistakes, and putting plans in place to keep performance at its best are all part of performance monitoring. By implementing these techniques, novices create a methodical approach to machine learning system management that goes beyond the creation of the initial model.

Establishing appropriate evaluation criteria to measure a model's performance is the basis for performance monitoring. The kind of task and the intended results determine which metrics are used. The coefficient of determination, or R-squared, which calculates the percentage of variance in the dependent variable that the model can account for, mean squared error, mean absolute error, and mean squared error are often used metrics for regression problems. These metrics shed light on how well the model predicts outcomes and how well it identifies underlying patterns in the data. The model's capacity to accurately identify examples, handle imbalanced classes, and prevent false positives or negatives is assessed using metrics including accuracy, precision, recall, F1-score, and the area under the receiver operating characteristic curve for classification tasks. Beginners may use performance monitoring without having to manually program intricate mathematical formulas, thanks to Python packages like scikit-learn, which offer built-in functions for efficiently calculating these metrics.

Since the properties of real-world data frequently change, it becomes crucial to monitor model performance over time when metrics are defined continuously. When the statistical characteristics of input features or goal variables change, a model trained on past data loses its predictive accuracy. This process is called concept drift. Seasonal changes, market trends, changing user behavior, and other outside variables can all cause concept drift. By examining changes in prediction distributions, comparing performance metrics on fresh data with past benchmarks, or examining input feature statistics, novices can keep an eye on idea drift. Learners can observe trends over time, spot anomalies, and spot patterns that might point to drifting data by utilizing Python visualization techniques with packages like Matplotlib, Seaborn, or Plotly. Through proactive performance monitoring, learners can update or retrain models in real time before predicted accuracy drastically drops.

Another crucial component of performance monitoring is error analysis. Although summary metrics give a general idea of how accurate the model is, they don't show the precise places where it isn't working well. To comprehend failure patterns, novices should look at cases that were incorrectly classified or had significant prediction errors. For instance, a classification model may frequently incorrectly classify a certain category as a result of overlapping feature traits or a lack of training instances. Examining these mistakes offers important information about the model's shortcomings, the caliber of the data, and possible enhancements. Beginners can thoroughly examine problems with Python tools like confusion matrices, categorization reports, and intricate visualizations, which help them gain a more sophisticated understanding of model behavior and direct specific improvements to boost efficiency.

Because it enables learners to grasp complex performance data intuitively, visualization is a key tool in performance monitoring. Trends, plateaus, or abrupt deviations can be seen by charting parameters like loss, accuracy, precision, and recall throughout training or operational periods. Regression models' residual plots, which show the variations between expected and actual values, can be used to spot outliers, heteroscedasticity, and non-linear correlations that could have an impact on performance. Scatter plots or multidimensional feature space visualizations can be used to show areas in classification models when the model has trouble differentiating between classes. Beginners may easily create understandable and instructive plots with Python's visualization packages, which enable them to track performance in real time and comprehend the connection between data, model behavior, and assessment criteria.

A crucial component of performance monitoring is testing the model on new data. Benchmarks such as holdout datasets or streaming data can be used to evaluate generalization and identify performance degradation. Learners may see whether predictions hold true, spot new trends, and decide whether retraining is required by routinely testing the model on fresh cases. Python's automated assessment pipelines make this process easier and allow for ongoing monitoring without the need for human interaction. Additionally, automation enables students to put alerting systems in place when performance indicators drop below predetermined levels, guaranteeing prompt action and preserving dependability in production settings.

Beyond accuracy measures, performance monitoring also takes operational factors like latency, throughput, and resource utilization into account. A model may generate correct predictions in production settings, but its sluggish inference times, high memory utilization, or excessive processing requirements may cause it to operate inefficiently. These elements should be taken into account by novices while tracking performance because operational inefficiencies can impact cost-effectiveness, scalability, and user experience. Learners may evaluate resource use and pinpoint bottlenecks with Python tools like time tracking functions, profiling modules, and logging frameworks, which help them strike a balance between predictive performance and usefulness.

Apart from these technical procedures, performance monitoring includes keeping an exhaustive record of model behavior, data modifications, and assessment outcomes. Reproducibility, accountability, and well-informed decision-making are all facilitated by clear documentation, especially in regulatory or cooperative settings. Python notebooks enable novices to follow model progress over time and facilitate communication of discoveries by combining code, metrics, visuals, and explanations in a single workflow. This process of methodical documentation and monitoring helps learners get ready for real-world applications and supports best practices in machine learning development.

To sum up, performance monitoring is an essential step for Python novices studying machine learning and artificial intelligence. By establishing measurements, monitoring changes over time, identifying errors, showing trends, assessing on fresh data, and taking operational efficiency into account, it guarantees that models will continue to operate accurately and dependably. Good monitoring aids in identifying idea drift, identifying flaws, directing retraining, and preserving prediction confidence. Gaining proficiency in performance monitoring helps students manage machine learning models in a methodical way, keeping them reliable, scalable, and useful in practical situations. This information gives novices the ability to create models and maintain their efficacy, laying a solid basis for more complex machine learning initiatives and the responsible application of AI.

Ethics in Artificial Intelligence

The moral, social, and legal ramifications of creating and implementing AI systems are the focus of the crucial field of artificial intelligence ethics research. Beginners must comprehend ethical issues to ensure responsible technology use as artificial intelligence becomes more and more ingrained in daily life, from healthcare and finance to transportation and entertainment. Examining how AI systems work, who benefits from them, and any potential unintended consequences is vital since these systems have the power to impact decisions that impact both individuals and society. Fairness, accountability, transparency, privacy, and preventing harm are all included in ethics in AI, which directs engineers to build systems that support human welfare and society ideals.

Fairness is one of the main ethical issues with AI. Data is used to train AI systems, and the knowledge they gain has a direct impact on the choices they make. The AI system may reinforce or even magnify prejudices present in the training data, whether they are the result of systemic discrimination, historical injustices, or the underrepresentation of particular populations. For instance, if previous hiring decisions were prejudiced, a recruiting algorithm trained on historical recruitment data can give preference to applicants of a specific gender or ethnicity. In order to guarantee that AI systems treat everyone equally, novices studying AI must comprehend the significance of assessing datasets for fairness, putting bias detection techniques into practice, and taking fairness metrics into account. Developing technology that does not perpetuate social inequalities requires this insight.

Another essential component of ethical AI is explainability and transparency. Numerous machine learning models, especially intricate ones like deep neural networks, are frequently referred to as "black boxes" due to the difficulty in deciphering their decision-making process. Beginners must understand that when AI systems affect human lives—for example, in financial approvals, legal decisions, or medical diagnoses—transparency is essential. Developers are able to comprehend and explain how models arrive at their predictions with explainable AI techniques, including feature importance analysis, local interpretable model-agnostic explanations, and visualization tools. Beginners can guarantee that AI systems offer insights that are comprehensible and accountable by emphasizing transparency, which will empower stakeholders to have faith in the technology and make wise decisions.

Another aspect of AI ethics is accountability. The choices AI systems make, and the results of those choices, must be the responsibility of developers, companies, and legislators. Clear documentation of the model's development, including its data sources, underlying presumptions, constraints, and testing protocols, is necessary for accountability. It also entails setting up systems for keeping an eye on AI systems that have been deployed and reacting to mistakes or unexpected results. Beginners should be aware that accountability encompasses governance, monitoring, and adherence to ethical norms in addition to technical implementation. By ensuring that stakeholders can recognize and resolve issues, responsible AI development shields people and communities from harm brought on by algorithmic mistakes or abuse.

Because AI models rely on data, which frequently contains private or sensitive information, privacy and data protection are crucial ethical issues. In order to handle data properly, beginners need to understand how to use techniques like encryption, anonymization, and secure storage. AI systems that abide by data protection laws, such as the General Data Protection Regulation, are guaranteed to respect people's right to privacy. Limiting data gathering to what is required, getting informed consent where appropriate, and preventing the exploitation of personal data are all further components of ethical AI development. Beginners may create technology that upholds user rights and promotes trust by incorporating privacy issues into the development and implementation of AI systems.

A larger ethical duty that takes into account societal impact, safety, and dependability is preventing harm. To prevent mistakes that could result in financial, emotional, or physical harm, AI systems need to be thoroughly vetted. For example, financial advice algorithms, medical diagnostic systems, and driverless cars can all have an impact on people's safety and well-being. The significance of risk assessment, thorough testing, and backup plans in the development process should be understood by novices. Long-term societal repercussions like employment displacement, social injustice, or the perpetuation of stereotypes must also be taken into account for ethical AI. By addressing these issues, AI systems can limit harmful effects and make a good contribution to society.

In AI ethics, accessibility and inclusion must also be taken into account. AI systems should be created with a variety of demographics in mind, avoiding the exclusion or disadvantage of any certain group. Learners should become proficient in assessing the representativeness of datasets, the accessibility of algorithms for users with varying skills, and the equity of deployment tactics. Instead of focusing benefits on a small group, inclusive AI makes sure that technology benefits a wide spectrum of people. It is possible for novices to design systems that support accessibility and equity by implementing ethical design principles early in the development process.

Lastly, AI ethics promote continuous introspection and learning. Artificial intelligence is developing quickly, and as technology gets more potent and widespread, moral dilemmas keep coming up. Beginners need to have an attitude of constant learning and keep up with new rules, case studies, and social discussions concerning artificial intelligence. The ethical implications of AI projects can be better understood by working with multidisciplinary teams that include ethicists, sociologists, legal experts, and domain specialists. Beginners may create ethical methods that guarantee AI systems are in line with human interests and social values by including ethics in every step of the machine learning workflow, from problem description to deployment and monitoring.

In conclusion, novices learning to create and implement machine learning systems must take ethics in AI into account. Fairness, accountability, transparency, privacy, harm prevention, inclusion, and ongoing reflection are some of the issues that help developers create trustworthy and responsible AI. By comprehending and resolving these ethical issues, AI technology can minimize dangers and adverse effects on people and society while yielding significant advantages. Beginners may lay a solid foundation for responsible practice by including ethical concepts in every level of AI development. This will enable them to successfully navigate the intricate and constantly changing field of artificial intelligence while making a good impact on society.

Navigating AI Success

Converting conceptual models into tools that add value in the real world requires an understanding of and commitment to an efficient AI process and deployment strategy. This chapter is important because it ensures that every choice, from problem definition to ethical considerations, leads to significant results by bridging the gap between theoretical AI design and workable solutions. With the right application, businesses and individuals may create AI systems that are precise, effective, and consistent with human values, which will enhance decision-making, operational effectiveness, and competitiveness. However, disregarding these guidelines may result in faulty models, skewed results, resource waste, and even harm to one's reputation. The practical implications are substantial: misaligned AI systems might cost businesses millions of dollars, poorly supervised models could jeopardize healthcare decisions, and if ethical issues are ignored, public confidence in technology could decline. Practitioners may traverse complicated AI projects with confidence and accountability by internalizing the principles learned in this chapter, which equips them with both technical expertise and strategic insight.

You will be able to articulate AI concerns in a way that is both user-friendly and in line with corporate objectives by the end of this chapter. You'll be able to create data collecting plans that optimize model performance while maintaining dependability and equity. You will comprehend deployment strategies that enable AI systems to function effectively at a large scale. You will be able to keep an eye on the model's performance and spot problems before they get out of hand. Additionally, you will be prepared to adopt ethical frameworks that protect against prejudice, abuse, or unforeseen repercussions.

Take the real-world example of a retail business using a recommendation engine. The business can prevent biased recommendations by properly articulating the problem (e.g., boosting customer engagement without encouraging biased product suggestions) and organizing data collection around a variety of user interactions. Constant observation guarantees that the engine adjusts to evolving consumer habits, and moral supervision guards against discriminatory or deceptive recommendations. Consider a small-town hospital using AI for patient triage in a brief example. After implementing the structured workflows from this chapter, the hospital restructured data inputs and monitoring systems, which led to faster and more accurate patient care. Initially, a poorly defined problem resulted in inaccurate prioritizing. This process can be compared to a gardener caring for a complex ecosystem: identifying the issue is like sowing the seed, gathering and analyzing data is like watering the soil, deploying the model is like sunlight assisting in its growth, and performance monitoring is like pruning to ensure healthy development. Ethics is like the protective fence that makes sure nothing dangerous spreads.

Clarify, Locate, Evaluate, Apply, Review is the CLEAR Framework that may be used to put these ideas into action right away. First, make the AI problem and its goals clear. Second, find the appropriate datasets and make sure they are high-quality. Third, consider deployment alternatives and possible moral ramifications. Fourth, use the model methodically while keeping an eye on how well it works. Lastly, iterate to increase accuracy, fairness, and utility by regularly reviewing the results.

Think about these five questions to increase comprehension and encourage useful reflection: In what ways does my present AI project support societal or organizational objectives? How can I lessen any biases that might be present in the data I intend to use? How will I assess the model's performance besides its accuracy? What moral conundrums might occur, and how can I anticipate and resolve them? Lastly, what actions can I take to guarantee that my AI system keeps developing responsibly as circumstances change?

Practitioners can improve their technical proficiency and cultivate a mindset that turns AI from a theoretical tool into a responsible, practical force with real-world impact by addressing these introspective questions and utilizing the CLEAR Framework.

CONCLUSION

The basic components required to start a meaningful journey into artificial intelligence are brought together in Stepwise Python Guide to AI and Machine Learning Beginners: Simple Explanations, Projects, and Workflows for Future Intelligent Software. This book turns difficult subjects into understandable information by fusing precise explanations with methodical learning procedures. In addition to being exposed to machine learning and programming ideas, readers are also led through real-world development process-inspired workflows.

You should gain greater confidence in your abilities to write Python code, manage data efficiently, and comprehend the development and assessment of intelligent models as you finish this guide. Throughout the book, some projects and examples show that AI is not just for professionals. Beginners may create useful models and systems that thoughtfully and creatively address real-world issues with time, effort, and curiosity.

This is just the beginning of the learning process. Rather, this book provides a solid basis for further investigation into more sophisticated algorithms, bigger datasets, and more intricate intelligent systems. You can continue to develop, explore, and contribute to the future of intelligent technology with competence, responsibility, and originality with the help of the Stepwise Python Guide to AI and Machine Learning Beginners.

Thank you for buying and reading/ listening to our book. If you found this book useful/ helpful please take a few minutes and leave a review on the platform where you purchased our book. Your feedback matters greatly to us.

www.ingramcontent.com/pod-product-compliance
Lightning Source LLC
LaVergne TN
LVHW022048200926
848481LV00003B/838